Read the Word:

The Bible Was Written For You

By Matthew Tague

PRESS

Cover art for this book was designed by Mike Gallardi
P.O. 6469
Oceanside, CA 92052
Email: info@mikegallardi.net

www.xulonpress.com

To my father and mother,
Who read the Bible to me every morning.
Because of your diligence, I am who I am.

Acknowledgements

This book is the result of people who have poured into me. Jesus is first because he is everything to me! Where would I be without my Savior? Knowing and serving him is the entire point of Scripture. You cannot read the Bible and understand it without knowing him.

For fifteen years my incredible wife Kelli has provided the type of home where I can devote time each week to studying God's Word and living it out. Her love has built the foundation for me to write this book. Her wisdom in the Word and her eye for detail in my preaching used to grate on me. Now they are my loving companions as I learn what it means to be a pastor. My dear children, Marli, Thaddeus and Annabelle have taught me what it is to be a father and have provided me more joy than a man should know. May you grow in the grace and knowledge of Jesus as you read this book.

My parent's, Steve and Renee Tague, dedicated many mornings to reading the Bible to me when I was young. Mom and Dad, I hope this book helps you in turn. Thanks for all that you poured into me.

A few teachers and leaders were instrumental to me in growing as a teacher of God's Word. Larry Peltier and Chris Olson first created in me a passionate desire to teach God's Word. Thanks, guys! Chuck Butler has been a constant companion and a source of pastoral wisdom for many years. Tom Blinco, Craig Cramblet and Ron Ohst have taught me more about the heart of God's Word than any class I ever took at seminary. Miles McPherson constantly pushes me to make sure that my preaching never loses touch with the average person. Because of these men, I am a better man. Whatever is helpful in this book is partially due to their influence in my life. If there are any mistakes, the credit is solely mine.

Karen Taylor spent many hours tirelessly editing this book. She knows it as well as I do. Any well crafted sentences are her creations! My great friend Mike Gallardi created the cover art for this book. Thank you, Mike for your friendship and for using your gifts for the lord

Lastly, Rancho del Rey Christian Church has provided an environment for me to teach and preach the Bible on a weekly basis for the last four years. The good people of that church will never know how much they teach me.

Table of Contents

Introduction

Did you ever hear the story about the king turned into a wild animal? Or the one about the army general who got leprosy? Or how about the story where a guy catches a fish, pulls a coin out of its mouth and pay his taxes with it? The Bible is FULL of stories like this.

I can't get over the Bible. It continues to startle and amaze me. It makes me laugh, makes me cry, gives me encouragement and convicts me of my sin. This shouldn't surprise me. If it really is God's Word to the human race, then it should be an emotional experience for me to read it. The more I learn from it and grow in it, the more it changes me.

Some Christians, however, just don't understand what I am talking about. They read but don't understand Bible translations written in old English. They don't grasp the meaning of the ancient ways of life in Bible stories. In many ways, people living in a rural Asian village today have more in common with the people in the Bible than most modern Americans. The western world has also reached the point where many adults did not participate in church or Sunday school as children. And let's face it, what would the average American rather do today? Read the Psalms or watch TV? All this leads many new Christians to say, "The Bible just doesn't make sense to me."

If this describes you, don't despair. The fact that you have picked up this book shows that you want to understand what the Bible is all about. This book is designed to help you in your quest.

God meant for Christians to *enjoy* the Bible, not just read it because he said to. As with anything in life, we most enjoy what we know something about. My hope is that this book will help you learn enough about the Bible to understand and apply its riches.

If you're already a student of the Bible, this book is also for you. Perhaps you want to grow in your understanding of the different forms of literature in the Bible, or you want to learn how to lead a Bible study. In this book you will find background material helpful in studying books of the Bible, cultural clues to look for when reading Scripture, and examples of how to understand the flow of biblical history.

The first chapter of this book explains the various kinds of literature in the Bible and why the Bible is arranged as it is. In the main body of the book, I seek to help you correctly interpret God's Word. This includes knowing the importance of context, culture and the like. Such awareness will give you more confidence in reading the Bible, which has come to us through ancient writers. If you have a better understanding of their way of writing and their view of the world, you will grasp more of their meaning. I've also included an appendix at the end of the book that explains how the books of the Bible got there in the first place.

The last chapter of this book provides tips to help you make spending time in God's Word an enriching daily habit. I have found that this is the least practiced and most needed kind of reading among Christians today. Since this is, or should be, a staple of the Christian experience, I have dealt with this last. Gaining a basic understanding of the Bible as a whole comes first, for it greatly enhances your devotional reading.

Chapter 1

An Overview of the Whole Bible

W hen I was young, there were magical days when my parents let me go to the local comic book store. I would save my money for a month and hold my breath as I waited to see what happened in the next issue of *Spiderman*, *Batman*, and *The Avengers*. I couldn't wait to get to the store and pick up the latest edition of each series. When we got home, I raced inside and spent the rest of the day in my room reading and living the adventures of each and every superhero. Man, what a life!

Now that I am grown up, I understand that excitement from a different point of view. When I wake up early in the morning and sit down with a cup of coffee, I can't wait to read what happens to Jeremiah or David or Jesus or Peter. I have read the Bible through countless times, and I still have a sense of wonder and awe as I read about the people in the Bible. God continues to bring out new aspects of his Word to me as I dedicate myself to reading and understanding it. He can do the same for you! Let's discover its riches together, shall we?

The Bible is a world-changing book. It begins in Genesis by tracing the history of a small group of ancient Middle Eastern people destined to change the world. It ends in Revelation with the prophecy of the King of Kings, Jesus, who will end world history by ushering in God's righteous kingdom. In between is the epic struggle of good versus evil, love and hate, law and disorder, truth and lies. It records the battles of God's people and their ever-changing relationship with the world as it accepts or rejects the message of God.

The Bible is a mind-blowing book, unique among all literature. It is a compilation of 66 books, spanning more than 1,500 years, written by more than 40 authors. Add that God himself superintended the process of these writings to such a degree that what the authors wrote was completely true in every respect — and it boggles the mind!

Even if you appreciate all this, however, it doesn't necessarily help when you sit down by yourself to read the Bible. It is important to understand not only that it was written by God and humans, but also that God used different methods of literary communication through these men. It is a common mistake to interpret the entire Bible in the same way. Doing so will cause frustration and confusion when you study the different sections of the Bible.

The first principle of biblical interpretation is to identify what kind of literature you're reading. You don't read a novel the same way you read a textbook or a blog, do you? It's the same with Scripture; knowing how to read correctly enhances your reading of it.

The Arrangement of the Books in the Bible

First, it's helpful to know why the books of the Bible are arranged as they are. The Bible consists of two major parts: the Old Testament and the New Testament. The Old Testament focuses mainly on the nation of Israel, God's plan for them in ancient history, and how through them, the Messiah of the world would come. The Old Testament contains thirty-nine books and makes up roughly two-thirds of your Bible. The New Testament focuses on the Messiah, Jesus. How he was received and what his followers did. The New Testament contains twenty-seven books and makes up one-third of the whole Bible.

Something good to remember is that the chapter divisions are *not* part of Scripture. Except for the book of Psalms, which is divided by "songs," the chapter divisions and verses in your modern translation were not in the ancient copies. They were added in the 1500's AD and later to make it easier for people to find what they needed in the Bible. The reason I point this out is that while the chapter divisions usually provide a reliable guide to natural stopping points in the text, once in a while they're not. Don't let chapter divisions limit you. If in your reading you sense that a story or a point continues beyond what the chapter divisions suggest, keep reading for yourself and gain the writer's point.

Within the Bible there are different types of writing. I will break down the major sections of both the Old and the New Testament's for you below.

The Old Testament

An easy way to remember the Old Testament's different kinds of literature in their correct order is to think *History, Poetry and Prophecy*. The Old Testament moves from telling us the story of the people of Israel, to recording the wisdom of that people, to giving us the prophecies of the ancient Israelites.

Old Testament History

The Old Testament is divided into sections. The first five books of the Bible are called the Torah (the Law) and were written by Moses. They are also known as the Pentateuch. They contain the record of the creation of the universe through the birth of the nation of Israel. These books also trace the deliverance of the Israelites from Egypt in the event known as the Exodus.

Since these books make up the earliest record of history from a Jewish perspective and also give the Law (summarized in the Ten Commandments) they are placed first. The books are **Genesis, Exodus, Leviticus, Numbers and Deuteronomy**.

The books that follow Deuteronomy detail what happened in Israel after the death of Moses in approximately 1500 BC until the nation of Israel returned from exile to the Promised Land (the Palestine area) in approximately 500 BC. These books are **Joshua, Judges, Ruth, I** and **II Samuel, I** and **II Kings, I** and **II Chronicles, Ezra, Nehemiah** and **Esther**. The events in some of these books take place outside of Israel. The story of Esther took place while the Israelites were exiled in a foreign land. While many of these books relate Israel's national and wartime events, not all do. The book of Ruth is an incredible story about one family from the town of Bethlehem.

A good Bible dictionary will identify the individual author and date each book of the Old Testament. Many study Bibles give brief informative introductions to each book of the Bible. They can be quite helpful in understanding an individual book.

Old Testament Poetry and Wisdom

After the historical books come the books of poetry and wisdom. Some Bible scholars separate these two categories. I have decided to combine them because some of the wisdom books contain beautiful poetry and the poetic books often teach wisdom. You'll see what I mean later when we dive into how to interpret these books. For now, just note that these books are located right in the middle of your Bible. The wisdom books are **Job, Proverbs** and **Ecclesiastes**. The books of poetry are **Psalms, Proverbs** and the **Song of Songs,** also known as the Song of Solomon.

Just because these books are grouped together doesn't mean they were written at the same time. The book of Job was probably written during the time Abraham lived (the account of Abraham's life is found in the book of Genesis), while Proverbs and Ecclesiastes were written about 900 BC, during the reign of King Solomon. The Psalms, a collection of prayers, songs and poems, were compiled over a period of time. Think of the poetry section of the Bible as the heart of the Old Testament. It expresses the emotions of the biblical characters in very real terms.

Old Testament Prophecy

The last section in the Old Testament contains the prophetic books. Some of these books also contain historical information about Israel, but their main purpose is relaying information about the future to the Israelites. The "major prophets" wrote four books and the "minor prophets" wrote thirteen books. "Major" and "minor" refer to length, not importance. The books of **Isaiah, Jeremiah** and **Ezekiel** are fairly long, each with more than forty-five chapters, so they're called the Major Prophets. The shorter book of **Lamentations** was included with the Major Prophets because it was written by Jeremiah. The Minor Prophets are much like the historical books in that they don't all necessarily cover events of the same importance from start to finish, and they don't all necessarily occur in historical order. Some of them are local in scope, some of national importance. Some authors were men of great influence, such as Daniel, whose name would have been known in many lands while he was alive. Others, such as Hosea, lived lives of relative obscurity, writing books whose messages still powerfully impact the reader today. The books of the Minor Prophets are **Daniel, Hosea, Joel, Amos, Obadiah, Jonah, Micah, Nahum, Habakkuk, Zephaniah, Haggai, Zechariah** and **Malachi.**

The New Testament

The New Testament is a collection of twenty-seven books written by nine men. The apostle Paul wrote thirteen letters, also called epistles, the apostle John wrote five books, the apostle Peter wrote two (and his experiences are behind a third, the Gospel of Mark, as we shall see later). Luke, a traveling companion of the apostle Paul, wrote two books. Just like modern literature, getting to know the authors helps us get to know their writing. We learn to understand their themes, their styles and their passions. In the end, these books were also written by the Holy Spirit, so God communicated everything we need for our lives as Christians, but he chose to do it through the writings of these men.

As we study the order of the New Testament books, the first thing to learn is that they exist as a collection of works, written by nine authors, placed in a logical order, beginning with the Gospels. The Gospels come first because they provide the basis for belief in Jesus and the foundation of the Christian faith. You can think of the order of the books in the New Testament this way: *Gospels, Letters, and Prophecy.*

The entire New Testament was written in what is called Koine Greek. This style of Greek was the common language of the Mediterranean world during the time that the Romans ruled. At that time, whether from Egypt, Spain, Turkey, or elsewhere, most people understood this language, so God ordained that the New Testament be written in the language read and understood by the majority of people.

New Testament Gospels and Acts

The New Testament begins with the life and ministry of Jesus of Nazareth recorded in the Gospels of Matthew, Mark, Luke and John. Jesus is the Messiah who came to earth to save the world from its sin. The Gospels focus on the events leading up to, during and after the crucifixion of Jesus. The synoptic Gospels, Matthew, Mark and Luke, tell the story of Jesus' ministry from similar perspectives. If you read these Gospels together, you notice they each mention many of the same events.

John wrote his Gospel from a different perspective, although he followed the same basic pattern as the other Gospels, starting with the ministry of Jesus and leading to the cross. There may be many reasons for John's different perspective, not the least of which is that he is identified in the Gospel as "the disciple that Jesus loved." He was one of Jesus' best friends. It's likely he had a chance to read the other three Gospels and wanted to include other events that happened in the life of Jesus. In fact, in **John 21:25** he notes, *"There were many other things that Jesus did, which, were every one of them to be written, I suppose that the world itself could not contain the books that would be written."* The Gospels end with the resurrection of Jesus.

The book of Acts, written by Luke, takes over from there. Acts picks up where the book of Luke ends. Jesus ascends to the Father and the disciples wait in Jerusalem for the Holy Spirit. Acts concludes almost thirty years later with the apostle Paul preaching the gospel in Rome, Italy. The book of Acts serves as a transition from the ministry of Jesus to the life of the Church which he began through the apostles.

Did You Know?

> **The New Testament letters are arranged
> by author and by length.
> Paul's are first because he wrote the most. His letters are
> arranged from longest to shortest; first come his letters to
> the churches, then his letters to individuals.**

New Testament Epistles

For approximately ten years after its formation, the Church's activities took place in and around Jerusalem with a single, growing body of believers. Once the Church began experiencing persecution, it rapidly spread to other areas and people outside the Jewish nation.

In every city they visited, the apostles and their followers went to the Jewish synagogues, the places where Jews worshiped God. They preached that Jesus was God's Son, citing the Old Testament texts that prophesied about him. Some of the people in each city put their belief in Jesus and then they started a church.

The churches in each city didn't consider themselves disconnected from the rest of the Church. Instead, they thought of themselves as meeting places for the members of the Church that lived in that particular area. The apostles wrote letters, called **epistles**, to different churches that they had visited or helped start, with helpful instructions about how to live their lives as Christians and how to conduct themselves in the world.

The person who wrote the most epistles to churches in Scripture is the apostle Paul. He wrote **Romans, I** and **II Corinthians, Galatians, Ephesians, Philippians, Colossians,** and **I and II Thessalonians.** These are the first epistles you come to as you read the New Testament. The reason they are arranged this way is that Romans is the longest and letters to the Thessalonians are the shortest in this group.

Many years later, when the Church began to organize the New Testament books into a single order, they put all of Paul's letters to churches in one group in order of longest to shortest. Then they placed Paul's letters to individual church leaders, **I and II Timothy, Titus,** and **Philemon**, again from longest to shortest.

The rest of the New Testament epistles follow Paul's letters. This group begins with the epistle to the **Hebrews**. There has been an ongoing discussion throughout Church history as to whether the apostle Paul wrote the book of Hebrews. It is similar in many ways to his other writings, but has some important stylistic differences. Ultimately, it doesn't matter too much who wrote Hebrews because the Holy Spirit is the divine author. It is clear, however, that the early Church thought Paul probably didn't write Hebrews because they placed it apart from, but next to, his other letters to the churches.

After Hebrews is **James**, written by the brother of Jesus, not the apostle James mentioned in the Gospels. That James, the apostle, died shortly after the Church began; he was killed by Herod because of his faith. James the brother of Jesus became a firm believer in Jesus after his resurrection, and served as a leader in the Jerusalem church for many years. The book of James is considered by many to be the "Proverbs of the New Testament" for the many wise sayings that it contains.

Following James are **I and II Peter**, by – you guessed it – the apostle Peter. It appears as if Peter wrote one of these books himself and then dictated the other to someone trained in writing. The style of the Greek language in one is rough and straightforward, as you would expect from the uneducated Peter we know from Scripture. The style of the other is more fluid and complex, as if it were written for Peter by someone called an amanuensis.

"Amanuensis" is a ten-dollar word meaning "someone who writes for you as you talk." Many writers in New Testament times had amanuenses. In fact, it seems Paul also used one when writing the book of Romans. He includes a sentence near the end of the book of Romans which reads, "I, Tersius, who wrote this letter, greet you in the Lord." **Romans 16:22**. Tersius is not another name for the apostle Paul; it is the name of another person! I cannot tell you how much consternation this passage of Scripture caused me from the time I was about twelve years old. Everybody always told me that Paul wrote Romans, but I read Romans and it said right there in **Romans 16:22** that Tersius wrote it. I thought there was some kind of big conspiracy or something. Imagine my relief when someone finally told me what an amanuensis was! Clearly, Paul dictated his letter to the Romans to Tersius.

Authors varied greatly in how much freedom they gave their amanuenses. Sometimes amanuenses had the freedom to change words and sentence structure and other times they were strictly to write what the author said. It all depended on the preference of the author. This process resembles how an employer might dictate a letter to a secretary today.

After Peter's letters come the letters of **I, II** and **III John**. John's first letter is similar in length to many of the other epistles, but II and III John are short and succinct, not even taking a whole page in most Bibles. You may read them and think, "Why did they put these in Scripture?" Besides the fact that they contain God-inspired messages about Christian living, we discover that everything the apostles wrote was VERY important to the early Church. They were the men who knew and witnessed the risen Lord Jesus.

The last of the epistles is from **Jude**, another brother of the Lord Jesus. Jude's message is similar to the book of II Peter, especially chapter two of II Peter. In fact, it is interesting to study the books side by side because they overlap so much. As with the Gospels, the information contained in Jude and II Peter is so important that the Holy Spirit gave it to us more than once. There are differences in emphasis between Jude and II Peter, but the two books taken together provide us with an interesting study in material that was important to the early followers of Christ. Christians have seen parallel material in the writings of Paul as well. Some of the things he wrote to the Ephesian church match almost word for word what he wrote to the Colossians. This helps us understand the model of the authors' writing and the themes that found their way to more than one congregation of God's people.

New Testament Prophecy

The last book in the New Testament is the book of **Revelation**, written by the apostle John. No book in the world has caused more arguments and false assumptions than this book. Don't let that turn you off, however; the book of Revelation is part of Scripture and greatly encouraging to Christians.

When we come to the section on interpreting Revelation, I will give you some help in how NOT to get off track in understanding the book. For now, it is important that you understand that Revelation appears last in the Bible for a few reasons. It records the last appearance of Jesus to an apostle. Jesus appeared to the apostle John when John was an old man, having been exiled to the Island of Patmos in the Mediterranean **Revelation 1:9**. Revelation also comes last because it is a prophecy of how Jesus will return to end world history as we know it. The message of the book of Revelation is this: *Jesus wins and God's Kingdom comes to earth in all its power.*

The book of Revelation is a prophetical book, having many things in common with the Old Testament books of prophecy. It also has similarities to a type of literature common in the time of Jesus called apocalyptic literature; you'll learn what that means later. Revelation is the final word from God to the followers of Jesus as we eagerly await his return to earth. It gives us hope and strength to continue our walk of faith, knowing that Jesus will return to earth and will one day cover the earth in his righteous reign.

Chapter 2

Some General Rules about Biblical Interpretation

B efore we start digging into each section of God's Word, I want to introduce you to a few points to aid your general study of God's Word, no matter what the kind of literature. Subsequent chapters deal with the specifics of each kind of literature in the Bible, but before we get there, it's important to keep these basic principles in mind. This serves as your Bible 101 class. These rules apply no matter what section of Scripture you study.

1. Remember, the Author Has a Point

Have you ever talked to someone who just won't get to the point of his story? It's one of the most frustrating things. You want to say, "Get to the point!" Most of the time, the goal of conversation is to communicate necessary information. Whether a business discussion between employer and employee, a casual conversation between two friends, or a doctor speaking to a patient, we talk because we have a point. The same is true of all writing.

Although the Bible was written thousands of years ago, the authors of Scripture believed that their writing was important and worth reading. Therefore, they had a point. When reading the Bible, you will find it easier to get the point of some sections than others. I encourage you to persevere even when it takes a while to discover the meaning. You'll be rewarded when you're done with a section or book and you understand the main point. You will begin to see all kinds of clues throughout the book that led you to the author's message. If you fail to keep in mind that the author has a point to convey, you will miss some important material.

In some portions of Scripture, the point is so easy to get that it doesn't require much work. The book of Proverbs contains many statements that are easy to understand and apply. Look at **Proverbs 11:12:** *"Whoever belittles his neighbor lacks sense, but a man of understanding remains silent."* The point is, "Don't say bad things about your neighbor. Instead, keep your mouth shut." Pretty easy conclusion, huh? Since Proverbs is a large collection of many smaller wisdom sayings, it's easy to work with when we want to find the point.

Many biblical books, however, take longer or reveal their point only at the end. The book of Ecclesiastes is a classic example. The author takes the reader down road after road of discussion, all of them seeming to lead to dead-ends. The last few verses of the last chapter, however, reveal the point. You may think, "Why didn't he just make his point and save everybody a lot of reading?" The reason is that you might not have gotten his meaning as clearly or might not have wanted to know his point as much had you not spent the time reading his illustrations about the matter.

Part of a good author's goal is to create the same thirst in you that compelled him to write his book. In Ecclesiastes, once you experience the writer's frustration, his anguish, his despondency with life, you begin to need the solution to the problem that he discovered. That way, at the end of the book, the solution satisfies you as it did him. He took you into his world, into his situation and you felt like he did. That is great writing.

Through his writing, the author of Ecclesiastes also lets the reader know that he thought through the whole situation and all the important possible conclusions. He meditated on the problem and tried to figure it out in many different ways.

Another reason for keeping in mind that the author had a point is that it keeps us focused on the details of the writing. Sometimes with the Bible, we skip details because we think, "I've heard this story before" or, having read one account in Matthew, we skip over the same account in Luke. But the good stuff is in the details. The more you look for the author's key message, the more attentive you are to the way the author weaves his story. Keep this statement in your head: *"What is this author's point?"*

2. The Analogy of Scripture

Suppose my wife said something strange to one of her friends, such as, "The dolphin is in the pool next to the Jell-O" and her friend asked me what my wife meant. I could do one of two things: try to explain what my wife really meant, always a dangerous thing for a husband to do, or tell the friend to ask my wife what she meant.

When my wife's friend asked what my wife meant, she would be going back to my wife at a different time in a different way. She didn't get my wife's point from their original conversation. By going back to the source for clarification, she will get the information she needs to understand my wife's unusual statement. This illustrates the *analogy of Scripture*, which teaches that the Bible is the best interpreter of the Bible.

The analogy of Scripture doesn't mean that *everything* in Scripture is explained by something else in Scripture. As a pastor, though, I have had innumerable experiences when some unclear concept in Scripture is explained by another, clearer, Scripture passage. Another name for this is "the analogy of faith."

Scripture itself is a wonderful resource for understanding other parts of Scripture. For instance, in **John 11:36-43**, Jesus hides himself from the Jewish leaders. The text tells us that even after Jesus did so many amazing things in front of them, they refused to believe in him. John quotes a few verses from the Old Testament book of **Isaiah 6:10**, then writes, *"Therefore they could not believe."* John weaves together an account of the Pharisees' unbelief in Jesus with an Old Testament prophecy that predicted the unbelief of the Pharisees. The Scripture in John 11 interpreted the Scripture from Isaiah. That's the analogy of Scripture working in an obvious way. **One author of Scripture explains what another Scripture means.** He makes the meaning clear for the reader.

The analogy of Scripture also works in less obvious ways. For instance, the epistle of I John reads, "God is light, and in him there is no darkness at all" **I John 1:5b**. The word "darkness" in I John is equivalent to "sin." It isn't a big theological stretch to link the words "darkness" and "sin" in John's writings. Therefore, when reading passages in the Old Testament that are hard to interpret or seem to make God the author of evil, it's helpful to remember the words of I John: *"God is light and in him there is no darkness at all."* Also consider **James 1:13:** *"Let no one say when he is tempted, 'I am being tempted by God,' for God cannot be tempted with evil and he himself tempts no one."* No one can look at a story in the Bible and say, "God wanted him or her to sin," because the New Testament makes clear that God never does that sort of thing.

That's the analogy of Scripture at work. The analogy of Scripture means using the books of the Bible together to interpret and understand God's Word more fully.

One final word about the analogy of Scripture: It's important to allow each book of the Bible to speak for itself. One passage of Scripture never "cancels out" another passage. Many portions of Scripture express things that are difficult for us to receive. We need to learn to accept and submit to them. There is a dynamic tension between systematically pulling together what the Scriptures say about a certain subject and allowing each book of the Bible to minister to us on its own. Never use the analogy of Scripture to distort or warp a legitimate lesson or point that God wants to teach you from a particular book of the Bible. Ultimately, a book-by-book study of the Bible will help you as you seek to put concepts together in Scripture. The two work hand in hand. Scripture never fights against itself. A truly biblical concept is one that is correct according to a single book of the Bible as well as consistent with what is contained in the entire Bible.

3. Original Meaning and Modern Application

When God used men to write the Bible, his Holy Spirit "carried" them along. They wrote total truth, but through the lens of their own life perspective. It was God writing, but it was them writing as well.

Scripture is unique in this characteristic. No other book can claim dual authorship with God.

The authors of Scripture wrote specific messages to certain people at a particular time in history, but God has used that writing to minister to and teach Christians for two thousand years. How does he do this? Nobody knows exactly. That's why the Bible is called inspired. It really is from God.

It's important for us to know and remember, however, that because the book of Romans, or Luke, or I Peter, was written to certain people in a certain time, **there's only one correct interpretation of what the author wrote to his audience.** There *cannot* be ten different and contradictory, yet correct, interpretations of a book of the Bible. The author meant to say something to his original audience. When you write a letter to someone, you usually want to convey some sort of information to them. It is no different with the Bible. The closer we get to understanding what the author's point was to his original audience, the closer we are to understanding the application God has for us.

When Paul wrote his letter to the Roman church, he addressed specific questions or issues that church had. The difference between the original context of the book, which was the Roman church in Paul's day, and the book's application to Christians, is that the original context means one thing only, while it can have many applications in our lives. Both are crucial to our understanding and learning. It's not correct to apply Scripture in any way we want, but it can be applied in multiple ways depending on the situation. For instance, Paul may say *"Don't let the sun go down while you are still angry"* **Ephesians 4:26**. This had one true meaning to his readers. As modern Christians, we are allowed to take that verse and *apply* it to a range of different situations, even outside of the original context. That's the difference between the original context and modern application.

God's Word has provided comfort, encouragement, conviction and strength for God's people through the past two thousand years. God applies his Word to us in many different ways, which is incredible.

The Point:

> **Scripture has one original context:** *One original point.*
> **Scripture has many subsequent applications:** *Many ways the text applies to our lives.*

The original context is the first thing you should try to find when you study the Scriptures. By getting at the original context, you're better able to correctly understand how the passage might apply to many different situations. If you don't understand the original meaning, it will be much harder to determine correct applications or how it fits into our modern situation.

When you study the Bible, it's important that you submit to what it says and not what you want it to say. In the book *An Experiment in Criticism*, C.S. Lewis wrote something about the great writers of the ages that I believe equally applies to biblical interpretation: "Find out what the author actually wrote and what the hard words meant and what the allusions were to and you have done far more for me than a hundred new interpretations or assessments could ever do."

4. Always Look for God

In a Nutshell:

> - **Look for what God is saying in the text through the author.**
> - **Look at how people in the text respond to him.**
> - **Look for the consequences of their actions as they obey or disobey him.**

Something that many people miss when they read Scripture is how God interacts with the people in the story. God is the principle actor in the Bible. His lines are the most important, and the story revolves around him. Therefore, whether you are studying history, prophecy, wisdom, parables, epistles, etc., you can learn by observing God in the passage.

First, look for what God says to the people in the passage. Does he encourage them, instruct them, correct them or rebuke them? As we read the Bible we learn what is close to God's heart when we reach deep and consider the things he loves and hates.

For instance, in the short book of Jonah, God asks Jonah to go and preach to the people living in Nineveh. At the time, Nineveh was the capital city of the Assyrian dynasty. Assyria was one of Israel's enemies. Knowing that, it doesn't take a great deal of thought to see why Jonah didn't want to go and preach a message of repentance to them. From this book, we see God's desire to save all people, not just the Israelites.

On a personal level, is there anything for modern Christians to learn from the account of God sending Jonah to share his plan with a group of people that Jonah detested? Yes. We learn that God loves even people we may despise. This can lead to all sorts of other applications for us.

Second, investigate how the people in Scripture respond to God. Do they accept his counsel? Do they respond in a half-hearted way? Do they listen to him? Do they want to follow the Lord's leading? Are they hesitant or courageous? When you take time to think about the different ways people in the Bible respond to God, you can clearly evaluate your own responses and where those responses will take you in your walk with God.

Returning to the story of Jonah, we see Jonah run from God's request and from God himself. Jonah continues to experience hardship and frustration when he runs from God's plan. In fact, he almost dies, yet the Lord miraculously keeps him alive and leads him to a place of submission.

Jonah's actions serve as a model of the kind of inner turmoil that believers experience when they run from God. In the Old Testament, we also see the opposite; courageous men and women accept the will of God for their lives and experience tremendous joy. Think of Daniel as he was lifted out of the lion's den. David struck down Goliath. Dozens of stories in the Old Testament give us courage to follow God's plans. It doesn't mean that things always turn out okay for us physically or circumstantially. It does mean that through it all, God is our joy and comfort.

Third, look at the consequences of people's actions. Are they rewarded? Do they encounter persecution? Are they encouraged? In the Old Testament, we see a clear pattern of blessing when people follow God's instructions and a pattern of hardship when they don't. As God blessed the Israelites materially when they followed the Lord's plans and kept his law, so he blesses us spiritually when we follow Jesus. In this way, you can apply the stories of the Old Testament by analogy. We are still blessed if we follow God, and suffer the consequences if we don't.

5. Understand the Different Kinds of Literature in the Bible

When my son was younger, he loved Lego's. More specifically, he loved a certain kind of Lego's called Bionicles. They're like robots, but with personalities. One of the coolest things about Bionicles is that you can buy one kit and build an individual Bionicle, but if you buy two or three kits of the same Bionicle, you can put all the pieces together to make an even bigger and better Bionicle.

As I considered how this fed my son's passion for Bionicles, I also realized that this is similar to the way the Bible is put together. Certain kinds of literature in the Bible fit together in a way that makes an integrated whole.

Take the Old Testament historical books. When you look at them together, you get the big picture of ancient Israel's history rather than the bits and pieces you get by reading the individual history books. All the groups of biblical literature taken together make an even bigger, more integrated book. How incredible!

When we study the individual sections of Scripture, we gain insight into the intricacies of how God expresses himself to us in poetry, history and prophecy. Yet when we put all of the sections together, we're able to see this remarkable construction by the Holy Spirit, the great Author of all Scripture. The Bible is truly an incredible work of God, so on our journey to make sense of the whole thing, we're going to break it down into its pieces, then put it back together.

As I wrote in the first chapter, the Bible is divided into different kinds of writing, usually grouped together for ease of reading. Just as you read a newspaper differently than you read a poem, you need to differentiate the various kinds of writing used in the Bible. In the Bible we find poetry, storytelling, history, prophecy, parables, philosophy, and more. No one would expect you to read a paper on philosophy with the same mindset as you would approach a piece of poetry.

That's the way it is with the different kinds of literature in the Bible. Some relay the facts of history in a straightforward way, while others appeal to the heart, and some do both at the same time. All are true and add to our understanding of God and his kingdom.

In the following chapters we will explore in detail the different kinds of literature in the Bible and some hints to help you read and understand them in their contexts.

**As we move to interpreting sections of Scripture,
keep these rules in mind:**

**1. The author has a point.
2. The analogy of Scripture: If Scripture explains something in another passage, let it.
3. While we can apply Scripture to our lives in many ways, the author only had one original meaning.
4. Always look for God in the Scriptures.
5. Understand the kind of literature you're reading within Scripture.**

Chapter 3

Old Testament History
Genesis - Esther, Jonah

My dad is a HUGE fan of San Diego State University football. When I was a kid, we went to the stadium every fall to watch the SDSU Aztecs play football. I still remember one game in particular, actually not one game, but one play. The Aztecs had the ball and were on their own twenty-five yard line. Their star running back had just been hurt, so they sent in a replacement, an untested freshman.

The first time they gave him the ball he cut to the left and ran more than seventy yards for a touchdown. I remember watching that play as though it unfolded in slow motion. I had a perfect view from the stands. I remember learning the player's name: Marshall Faulk. He went on to run more than two hundred yards that game and single-handedly brought excitement to the SDSU football program for three years. He ended up playing professional football in the NFL and became one of the best running backs ever. I don't remember a lot about the SDSU program in those years, but I do remember that first run by Marshall Faulk.

Some of the history recorded in the Bible is a little bit like this Marshall Faulk story. It isn't all-encompassing or complete from a historical standpoint. Genesis through Esther focus on specific events in the nation of Israel as individuals followed God's leading.

Each event recorded is true and did happen, yet it isn't a total record of everything that happened in Israel from 1200 B.C. to 400 B.C.

Understanding the Historical Sections (Stories) of Scripture

Biblical stories from both the Old and New Testaments have two aspects that are important to understand as we seek to correctly interpret them. Biblical scholar Grant Osborne wrote a seminary textbook called *The Hermeneutical Spiral* that outlined the two main aspects of a biblical story.

> **Historical Aspect** – This gives you the information in a factual way. What happened when and to whom?
> **Literary Aspect** – This gives you the author's message about the facts. This is how the author chooses to tell the story.

Since both the Old and New Testament contain stories, some examples in this section will be drawn from the New Testament.

1. Historical Aspect

Like the beautiful diamond ring I hope to buy my wife someday for our anniversary, the historical aspect of Scripture has many sparkling facets to be aware of as you seek to understand the Bible. The study of history has greatly added to our knowledge of scripture. The following points should help you as you seek to grow in your understanding of the history of the Old Testament.

A) Geography
Did you know that getting a parking space at the local mall at Christmastime is exactly like building an ancient city? It's all about the spot you get. If you get a primo spot right near the front, you're really happy.

In the ancient world, a good water supply, a defensible position and control of the local territories were key factors in building a city. Geography played a huge role in the ancient world. Ancient peoples situated their empires and kingdoms near strategic places of commerce and trade routes, as well as near water supplies and defensible positions. One of the reasons that Egypt remained a dominant Middle Eastern power for so long is that it could only be attacked from one direction and even that was challenging.

I encourage you to familiarize yourself with the geography that connected the ancient Middle Eastern world. Look at how the locations of Assyria, Babylon, Greece, Rome and Egypt related to Israel. Learn the territories of Israel that were assigned to the twelve tribes. Know the location of the Jordan River and Jerusalem.

Simply studying the maps at the back of a good study Bible is very useful. Most include maps of the Mediterranean world, the Palestine area and the whole Middle East, arranged by the time periods in the Bible.

Did You Know?

> **What we call a hill, the ancient Israelites called a mountain;**
> **What we call a desert, they called the wilderness.**

One important point to understand about geography in Israel is what they saw as a mountain is a hill to us, and what they called a hill is to us a mound of dirt. Israel is a hilly country, and when the Old Testament describes Jerusalem as surrounded by mountains, it's more like a series of hills. In America, we have two huge mountain ranges, the Rocky Mountains in the west and the Appalachian Mountains in the east, so we have a different mindset about mountains than the Israelites did.

Along similar lines, when the Scriptures use the term wilderness, it means the desert. When most Americans hear the word wilderness, we picture forests. In the ancient Middle East, the wilderness consisted of the vast regions of desert and rocky places away from rivers, lakes and populated areas.

B) Military and War

A major portion of biblical history has to do with which nations controlled the ancient Middle East and for how long. Sometimes new techniques of warfare helped tremendously in winning major battles. Other times, circumstances beyond anyone's control decided a battle. Political, economic and cultural struggles found their focal point during military campaigns.

Understanding that the Romans enjoyed military dominance over the Greeks but incorporated the Greek language and culture explains why the first-century person probably spoke Greek instead of the Roman language, Latin. Familiarity with the military gear Roman soldiers wore in New Testament times is a great help in interpreting the "armor of God" in **Ephesians 6:10-20.** Knowing the responsibilities and rank of a Roman centurion increases your understanding of the New Testament Gospel stories that mention centurions.

To better understand Old Testament battles, you have to appreciate the protection that a walled city provided. Each geographical area likely had what biblical authors called a fortified city. A fortified city is nothing more than a large city with a fortress encircled by strong walls. These walls protected the inhabitants from marauders and attacking armies. The strength of a fortified city, however, was also its weakness. Once the citizens of a certain area went inside, the attacking army could surround it and start a starvation campaign against it. The people in a fortified city needed to store months of food and water supplies in order to hold out against attack.

The Old Testament depicts many attacking armies coming against the walls of Jerusalem. Ancient people devised many weapons and tools for the defense of their city as well as for attacks on the walls of other cities. City walls were their primary mode of defense against invasion and their primary target of attacks against other nations.

C) Cultural and Social Practices

Another key to understanding many stories in the Old Testament is appreciating that the concepts of honor and shame were central to the ancient mind. Respect in the sight of one's peers and elders was of utmost importance. Not allowing one's family name to be dishonored or shamed was also of the highest concern.

The concept of honor runs implicitly through many Old Testament passages. Bargaining for a wife, or retaliation and warfare in response to minor insults may seem strange to us, but once you recognize the underlying concepts of honor and shame, some puzzling passages become clearer.

Take, for instance, the story in **II Samuel 10:1-5** where David's friend, the Ammonite king Nahash, has just died. David sends ambassadors in a gesture of good will to the new king, Nahash's son Hanun. King Hanun's advisors convince him that David actually sent the men as spies, so Hanun orders his men to cut off half the beard of each man. Hanun also cuts off their garments at the hips and sends them away half naked.

If this happened today, it would be extremely embarrassing, but in the ancient world the humiliation was probably worse than killing David's ambassadors. David likely received the news about his ambassadors with the following emotions and thoughts:

- You treated my friendship with your father with contempt, thereby breaking faith with your father and his memory.
- You dishonored my gesture of goodwill.
- You refused to honor my power as a greater and more powerful king.
- You shamed my ambassadors, sending them away naked and beardless (the two most physically shameful things that could be done to a man).
- You showed no respect for your ancestors and their alliances.

At this point, David had no choice as a king but to regain honor by ruthlessly destroying this Ammonite king. David's culture and sense of self-respect would not tolerate such humiliation by another king. David's ambassadors were commanded to hide themselves in an outlying village until their beards grew back, *"for they felt deep shame because of their appearance."* **II Samuel 10:5**

In the ancient Middle East, honor and shame dominated almost every social interaction. Every person tried to gain honor every way they could. A man or woman could gain honor in their family, extended family, village, city and nation. There was never a time when the concept of honor was out of sight. People gained honor by success. Success came in a variety of ways. For men it included gaining wealth, bravery on the battle field or strict religious observance. For women it came mostly through child bearing, especially bearing male children, and through faithfulness to her husband. Honor was the thing to get.

The reverse is also true. If one did not gain honor, they gained shame. A person could be shamed within their family, extended family, village, city or nation. Shame was accumulated by not having children, by exhibiting cowardice, or by disregarding the law. People exerted themselves to gain honor and to stay away from shame.

Knowing this helps us understand why Joseph was treated so poorly by his older brothers when he had dreams of them bowing down to him in Genesis 37. Joseph was a favored child of his father Jacob even though he was the eleventh born son. This was unheard of in ancient times. Usually it was the oldest son who received the most affection from the father. To make matters worse, Joseph had a dream that all his older brothers, along with his mother and father, were bowing down to him. He even had the audacity to share this dream with all of them!

In today's world, if a younger brother told his older brothers that they will bow down to him, they may be insulted, but that's about it. Back then however, if a younger brother told his older brothers that they would bow down to him, it was time to put him in his place. You or I may think of selling Joseph into slavery as extreme, (and it was!) but Joseph's older brothers were desperately trying to avoid the continual shame of having a prideful younger brother who was always treated better by their father. They sold him into slavery to get rid of him and regain their honor and status in their father's eyes. Yet they told his father that he was killed by wild animals to avoid the shame of him knowing that they sold their own brother into slavery.

D) Religious Customs

Knowing the religious climate of the Israelites and their enemies gives you valuable insight as you read the Bible. This sometimes gives insight into why God acted a certain way at a certain time, depending on who Israel was at war with.

Familiarity with the Egyptian gods helps one discern why God sent specific plagues against them in Exodus. Here are two examples: The Egyptians worshiped the Nile River. When God turned the Nile River to blood, it was a powerful symbol to the Egyptians that the Hebrew God was stronger than their gods. The Egyptians also worshiped frogs. When their land was invaded by frogs, it was a sign that their gods were not as powerful as the Hebrew God who could send frogs to invade their land.

A basic understanding of the gods of the Philistines, Assyrians, Babylonians and Canaanites will also prove valuable as you read the Old Testament. An easy way to get this information is to pick up a good Bible encyclopedia or dictionary. Looking up the word "Canaanite" will tell you a lot about the Canaanites' religion and way of life. In this way, you will grow in your understanding of the ancient world and in your ability to better understand and explain Scripture.

2. Literary Aspect

The literary aspect of a story tells us HOW the author relates his story. It gives the author's perspective, what he chooses to emphasize in his account of a historical event. The literary aspect is easier to find in the New Testament Gospels than in the Old Testament. For instance, since we have four Gospel accounts of the life of Jesus, it is easier to determine a certain author's focus in relaying the material because we have three other versions to compare it to.

This section will point out clues in the biblical narratives that make it easier to determine the author's point. Every author chooses how he will tell a story, focusing on certain details at the expense of others.

When we look to the Gospel of Luke, for example, we see that it tends to focus on Jesus' ministry to Gentiles, women, the poor, etc.

It seems that Luke wanted to make sure he included details of how Jesus interacted with these groups of people.

Knowing Luke's focus is important because Luke was probably an educated Gentile himself, part of the early Christian community. He wanted to show that Jesus came as the savior of the whole world, not just of the Jewish nation. Therefore, this emphasis comes out in his Gospel, guided by the Holy Spirit, yet written through his unique perspective.

So remember, this section is about *how* the author tells his story. As you learn to discern the how, you start getting lots of information about the *why* of the author's story as well.

A) Don't Overlook the Obvious

The Bible does give obvious clues to its meaning or purpose at times, and we shouldn't overlook those. Always take what a biblical author writes at face value, as his real meaning. For instance, in **John 20:30-31** the author is clear that he wrote his book so his readers might believe that Jesus is the Christ. Whatever other information or meaning we might find in a book of the Bible, we know that the overall purpose of a book will conform to any explicit purpose the author gives.

The Bible does not contain hidden meanings beneath its own stated purpose. While we can always find great "nuggets" of meaning in a biblical book, they will never come at the expense of the book's main purpose. If we think we find "insights" from books of the Bible that go against the clearly stated purpose of those books, we're mistaken in our interpretation.

B) Identify the Author's Intended Audience

Since the Bible is God's Word to all people, he intended it for a group larger than the original audience. Nevertheless, it was also given first to a certain group of people to read at a certain time; that's called the original audience.

For instance, in **Ruth 4:18-22**, the author gives his audience a genealogy that ends with King David. This tells us at least two things: first, the book was written after King David had become famous, many years after the events in the book happened. Second, it tells us that the audience was Jewish because non-Jewish readers would not have cared about someone named "David, the son of Jesse." By paying attention to the details, we've just learned two things: the general time frame the author wrote the book and who his audience was.

Another way of finding the audience is to notice words that the author translates or doesn't translate for his readers. It helps us begin to narrow down the options of who the author was writing to. Take the Gospel of John again. In **John 1:38**, Jesus' disciples call him "Rabbi," which John translates for his readers: "Rabbi (which means teacher)..."

Again and again, John translates the most general Jewish terms for his audience. Therefore, it's safe to assume that his audience wasn't Jewish. John would never have translated the Hebrew word "Rabbi" for Jewish readers. They knew what "Rabbi" meant.

As always, remember not to overlook the obvious, because many times a biblical author reveals his original audience in the opening to his book. On most occasions, Paul addresses the individual or church he is writing to by name. Luke also does this in his Gospel and in Acts.

C) Look for Repetition

Biblical authors repeat themselves for emphasis just as modern authors do. In his Gospel, John often quotes Jesus saying, "I am" on numerous occasions. "I am the bread of life...," "I am the door...," "I am the good shepherd." This helps us understand John's point. It was important to him to stress the titles Jesus gave himself that make it clear he is the only way to salvation.

A repeated theme in the parables of Jesus is "The Kingdom of God" or "The Kingdom of Heaven". Matthew, Mark and Luke spend a significant portion of their books dealing with this theme. Each author stresses the importance of the kingdom of God in his unique writing style. For instance, Matthew calls it "The Kingdom of Heaven" because he's writing to Jews and it was offensive to them to utter or write the actual word "God." Although Matthew changes the title slightly, we see that this concept was very important in Jesus' teaching.

In Genesis 1, Moses, the author, uses repetition to tell the story of the beginning of the world. There could be many reasons why he chose to do this. When you read the chapter out loud, it feels like he wants it to be easy to memorize. That could be one reason for the repetition. Genesis 1 is a good example because the repetition of "God said…and it was so…and God called it good" is so clear. Read Genesis 1 and count how many times those and other phrases are repeated.

D) Read It Many Times In Various Translations

Reading Scripture in a variety of translations helps you to get a better grasp on the meaning of a particular verse. The more you read something, the more likely you are to understand it. Sometimes a different translation helps you with a concept you found difficult in another.

If you're unsure of the meaning of a particular verse, read it in good translations such as the New Living Translation, the New International Version, New American Standard Bible and the English Standard Version. These modern translations are all reliable records of the inspired Word of God. God has blessed the Church with many trustworthy and knowledgeable men and women who have accurately translated the Word of God from the original languages.

E) Check with a Good Bible Dictionary or Bible Encyclopedia

A Bible dictionary or encyclopedia will give you as much or more information than you want about a particular subject. Let's say you want information on the Philistines. Reading an article about the Philistines from a good Bible dictionary will enhance your reading of any story that involves the Philistines in the Old Testament.

A search like this usually yields immediate results in your understanding of the text. Always remember, however, that while the editor's or author's opinion on a subject may be well informed, it isn't always correct. You need to sift the information for yourself and see how it fits within the context of the passage you're reading.

As you read the stories of Scripture, learn to pick out the historical and literary details. The more you investigate the details of each story, the better you will become at this process. You might not even remember the words "historical aspect" and "literary aspect," but you'll intuitively think about the details of the story and why they're included.

Chapter 4

Old Testament Law
Exodus – Deuteronomy

Once, when I was a senior in high school, my friends and I decided to go out and have some good "clean" fun. We picked up about 100 rolls of toilet paper from the local grocer, waited until about 10:00 in the evening and then set out to fulfill our creative destinies.

One of my friends brought along some firecrackers. (We never were very smart.) As we finished up toilet papering a house, one of the guys lit some of the firecrackers to wake up the household to behold our work. Then we drove off into the night.

As we were in the middle of toilet papering the fifth house, we heard sirens. All of a sudden three police cars roared through the neighborhood and came screaming down on us. Most of us froze right where we were.

One of my friends, however, who grew up on the wrong side of the tracks, immediately ran. Following suit, I ran, too, as did most of the group. We ran through neighborhoods, over fences, and through people's backyards with the officers chasing us.

We finally hid behind some bushes in the front yard of a house. The police officers came by about five minutes later and spotted one of us. They began picking us out of the yard one by one. For some reason, they missed three of us. We crouched under the bushes for another ten minutes, holding our breath, as our friends were taken away in the back of police cars.

We found out later that the police officers escorted each of them home to some very angry parents. I, however, along with two friends, did not get caught. We waited until the police drove off, and then hightailed it to one friend's house, and he drove us home.

Even though I didn't get caught, that was my last experience toilet papering on a large scale. Just seeing my friends carted off in a police car was enough to keep me on the straight and narrow. The presence of the law showed me what I was to do and not to do.

Although the stakes were much higher in ancient Israel, the analogy still holds true. When God delivered the Israelites from the Egyptians and led them to the Promised Land, he gave them a set of standards to live by. The standard is summarized in the Ten Commandments found in **Exodus 20:1-17** and again in **Deuteronomy 5:6-21.** In addition to the Ten Commandments, numerous laws in Exodus, Leviticus, Numbers and Deuteronomy cover everything from major crimes to sacrifice issues to how to dress. God gave these laws and rules to the Hebrews to teach them right from wrong.

What is the modern-day Christian to make of these rules? Does God expect us to follow the directions in Leviticus 14 for scraping leprous diseases off the walls of our homes? Most of us would agree that it's God's will for us to follow the Ten Commandments, but what makes the rest of the law different?

The answer is found in Jesus and something called the *new covenant.* Jesus said that he did not come to abolish the law but to fulfill the law, **Matthew 5:17.** He told us that we are part of a new covenant with him because of his death on the cross for us, **I Corinthians 11:25.** Jesus knew that we couldn't follow the law on our own, so he fulfilled it for us.

Once we're saved and filled with the Holy Spirit, we are empowered to follow the dictates of the Spirit, against which, **Galatians 5:23** tells us, *"there is no law."* We're free to live as God wants his children to live. It just so happens that the Ten Commandments summarize how he wants his children to live. So when we follow the Holy Spirit, we follow the Ten Commandments as well.

For the Christian, following God's law doesn't mean just doing the right thing, but having a godly attitude as well. Jesus spent a lot of time in Matthew 5 teaching that it isn't only the outward conformity to the law that justifies a person, but inward obedience. He says, *"You have heard that it was said to those of old, 'You shall not murder; and whoever murders will be liable to judgment.' But I say to you that everyone who is angry with his brother will be liable to judgment"* **Matthew 5:21-22a**. The law can never teach inward obedience; only the Holy Spirit can do that.

Part of God's purpose in giving us the law was to show us how deeply sinful we really are. Paul says in **Romans 7:7** *"In fact, it was the law that showed me my sin. I would never have known that coveting is wrong if the law had not said, 'You must not covet.'"* This way, when the New Testament explains that Jesus is the final sacrifice for our sins, we should embrace him, knowing that we could never fulfill the law ourselves.

In ancient Israel, the law existed not just for moral and religious purposes, but for social and cultural purposes as well. This was because God served as their king as well as their God. In other words, God was their military and political ruler as well as their religious law giver. Once you understand the Old Testament law as a whole, you can study the different kinds of laws contained in the Old Testament and their relevance for then and now.

Did You Know?

> **God gave three kinds of laws in Exodus through Deuteronomy.**
> **Moral laws: The Ten Commandments, to be followed by all people at all times. Example: Exodus 20:1-17**
> **Religious/Cultural laws: Rules for the worship of God in Israelite homes, society and the tabernacle. Dietary laws, dress codes and cleanliness laws.**
> **Example: Leviticus chapters 1-7**
> **Civil laws: The political and police laws for the ancient Israelite nation.**
> **Example: Leviticus 24:17-23**

Even though not all the laws in the Old Testament were as important as the Ten Commandments, we can still learn from all of them. It's important to realize that God gave the Hebrews different laws for different reasons. Some laws had to do with their worship of God. Some laws had to do with civil order, since God was not just a religious figure to be worshiped, but also their ruler to be obeyed. Other laws had to do with cultural issues that would make the Jews distinct from the nations around them.

Imagine that because of some sort of crisis, your extended family of thirty people was going to share one home. You would need to set up rules for acceptable conduct in the home, doing chores, who gets which rooms and why, etc. The situation was similar when the Israelites moved into the Promised Land. God was their patriarch and he gave them guidelines for proper living. If they were all going to live together in peace, somebody had to set the boundaries.

God was specific. For instance, the religious rules included detailed instructions on preparing sacrifices for worship. The civil laws told what to do when someone unintentionally killed another person. God even gave rules to the Israelites for how to get mold out of their homes (remember that God was dealing with an ancient group of people that didn't have Lysol). Those rules were both civil and cultural. Many civil rules that God instituted may seem trivial to us but were vital in a culture without modern hygiene and sanitation practices. Without such rules, deadly diseases and plagues could spread rapidly under certain circumstances.

Moral Rules

The Ten Commandments still govern our Christian behavior today. God wrote them on tablets of stone and gave them to Moses on Mt. Sinai. They outlined timeless principles of right behavior for humans. Paul even referred to them as "the law" in Romans 2.

Even tribal people who don't have a written copy of these laws recognize their rightness when they make their own laws. C.S. Lewis pointed out in his book *The Abolition of Man* that most cultures have similar moral structures. They happen to closely resemble the Ten Commandments.

In most cultures, commands such as "honor your ancestors, do not murder, do not commit adultery, and do not steal" find their way into the important tribal customs. Exceptions exist, of course, but C.S. Lewis also dealt with those. Anyone interested in better understanding natural law or moral law would do well to read *The Abolition of Man.*

These moral rules are the laws that all people should follow at all times. It's easy to see the wisdom of these rules when you think about basic human conduct. In the Ten Commandments we find four rules pertaining to the worship of God and six rules outlining behavior toward other people.

The rules for worshiping God are simple. We are not to worship any other god. We are not to make an idol or an image of God. We are not to use the Lord's name in a profane way, and we are to honor the Sabbath.

The last six of the Ten Commandments are also simple. Jesus summed them up when he said, *"And whatever you would want others to do to you, do to them."* **Luke 6:31.** In a nutshell, these six commandments tell us to honor our parents, don't murder, don't commit adultery, don't steal, don't lie and don't covet anything that belongs to anyone else.

Think of the Ten Commandments as a basic summary of the entire Old Testament law. They are the basic rules of living for all people at all times. Like I said earlier, Jesus died for us because we could never fulfill the requirements of the law. But once we are saved, God gives us the power to live in obedience to the moral law which can be summed up in Luke's Gospel as, *"Love the Lord your God with all your heart...and love your neighbor as yourself."* **Luke 10:26-28**. If we do this, we will be following the Ten Commandments. We can't do this perfectly, but we are now free to pursue it with all our hearts, without the guilt of feeling that we can never measure up to it. Jesus takes care of our sin and we gain his power to do what is right.

Religious/Cultural Rules

You've probably heard the saying, "cleanliness is next to godliness." That phrase describes the culture of ancient Israel and the rules governing how the people were to worship God.

As I mentioned earlier, God provided detailed rules governing how to worship him. The people were to do certain things and not do others. They were allowed to offer certain kinds of animals but not others. They had to make sure they were ceremonially clean before any worship activity. God knew that washing their hands did not ensure their hearts were clean. Nonetheless, it was important for the Israelites to go through the rituals of cleanness in order to understand that their God was a holy and righteous God. He would not stand for any stain or impurity of sin.

Such rigorous rules kept the Israelites from getting lax in their worship of God. God ordained levels of purity and service. For instance, all the Israelites were God's chosen people, but from the twelve tribes, God chose only one tribe, the Levites, to minister to the Lord in the tabernacle. Then, from the Levites, he chose one specific family, the family of Aaron and Moses, to serve as priests.

Therefore, although God included all Israelites in his covenant, he prescribed a certain way of doing things. The Israelites needed to learn that they could approach God only in the specific ways he directed. Every time the Hebrews questioned this, God rebuked them.

Before you skip the laws that instruct which parts of animals could be used in sacrifice and which were to be discarded, consider that God provided for the priests and their families through the sacrifices that the people brought. For each sacrifice that was brought, a portion was given back to the family to eat and a portion was given to the priest for him and his family. Although such Scripture passages may not be the most interesting to us, when we do read them, we learn how God took care of the priestly families. This is an example of how we can learn from all of God's laws...

Included in the religious/cultural laws are rules for how God wanted the people to dress. The men had to look a certain way and the females had to look a certain way. This was to distinguish them from the nations around them since they were God's special people.

The men had to trim their hair in a certain way and the women had to clothe themselves in a certain way. This was not only for modesty sake, but for the sake of helping them realize that God was even in charge of their appearance. God was the supreme authority over every area of their lives.

The Civil Rules

God gave the civil rules in the Old Testament to keep law and order in Israeli society. Think of these rules as crimes and misdemeanors. As I mentioned earlier, God served as the Israelites' king. He gave them rules for the punishment of minor offenses and major offenses. As you read, you will be able to see that God was not malicious or uncaring. In Numbers 35, he even goes so far as to give places of refuge to people who may have killed someone accidentally. God knew that that the dead man's family might still want justice against the person who accidentally killed their relative, so God provided cities that existed for the purpose of harboring someone who had committed a crime unknowingly.

Eventually the Israelites disobeyed God and asked for a human king of their own so that they could be like the other nations around them. God told the prophet and priest Samuel in **I Samuel 8:7,** *"And the Lord said to Samuel, 'Obey the voice of the people in all that they say to you, for they have not rejected you, but they have rejected me from being king over them."* It's interesting to know that even after they made a king for themselves, the Jews continued to follow many of the civil laws that God had instituted.

It's good to understand God's dual role as both God and king of the Hebrews. When God meted out a punishment for a crime or disobedience to his laws, it was for a specific reason and purpose.

In summary, whenever you read a law in the Old Testament that describes the punishment for a crime or how a person should treat others, you can assume that this is one of the civil laws.

As you learn to discern the different kinds of Old Testament laws, you will be well on your way to understanding the reasons for those laws and the structure they created for the ancient Israelites, morally, civilly and religiously.

Chapter 5

Wisdom Literature
Job, Proverbs, Ecclesiastes

I have an old friend named Tom. He's an eighty-year-old retired missionary who served in Central America. He also happens to be from Scotland. Whenever we get together, he never fails to give me good biblical wisdom, but he also makes me laugh. His old sayings and common sense combine with a deep sense of the Holy Spirit and biblical thought, all delivered in a delightful Scottish accent. What more could I ask for? It's like having a Christian Sean Connery as a personal mentor.

I've gained much from our friendship through the years. Tom reminds me of the wisdom literature of the Bible. The Bible's wisdom comes from a deep well of spiritual truth, and it makes sense on both spiritual and practical levels.

Biblical wisdom literature is broken up into two categories. The first is along the lines of "wisdom to live by," and contained in Proverbs. The second kind gets into philosophy and includes lengthy arguments about the deep questions that people of all ages have asked. Such questions as "Why do bad things happen to good people?" and "What is the meaning of life?" are addressed in the books of Job and Ecclesiastes.

Proverbs

The wisdom literature of the Bible is called "wisdom" litera-ture for a reason. It's wise advice. I read Proverbs continually. I read a chapter of Proverb each day corresponding to the date of the month. Since Proverbs has thirty-one chapters, this works out to reading almost all of Proverbs each month. I can't tell you how many times I've read them, yet I gain new and greater wisdom each time I read them. I recommend that when you read Proverbs you "soak it in." Memorize specific proverbs. Find new ways of stating these ancient proverbs. Learn to speak the language of Proverbs in modern English.

The book of Proverbs is similar to other ancient wisdom litera-ture found in the Middle East at the time it was written. What sets Proverbs apart from other wisdom writings of the time is the frequent admonition that *"The fear of the Lord is the beginning of wisdom,"* i.e., **Proverbs 1:6**. The point behind the Proverbs is that while life brings many different circumstances, learning how to live the right way ultimately is found in centering one's life on the worship of God.

BEWARE, however, of deriving promises from the wise counsel of Proverbs. Some Christians take Proverbs as a book where God promises that if you do good, good things will happen to you each and every time. That's not God's intent. Proverbs is an "everything being equal, it's better to do this" kind of book. It's meant to give guidelines for living a wise life. Keep that in mind as you read it.

For instance, **Proverbs 26:18-19** reads, "Like a madman who throws firebrands, arrows and death is the man who deceives his neighbor and says, 'I am only joking!'" This is general counsel. Have there been times when a man has deceived his neighbor and both have had a good laugh about it? Sure. The point of this proverb is to give a general warning. It's not intended to be taken in an "every time, throughout history" sense.

Did You Know?

> **The Proverbs do not give specific promises**
> **but *general wisdom***
> ***that, if followed, usually leads to good results.***

Most of the proverbs are simple, direct and easy to remember. They're pithy sayings. Remember the adage, "A bird in the hand beats two in the bush"? It's similar to many of the proverbs. They're designed to be easily digested.

Sometimes the proverbs use a literary device that states things twice in different ways to get the same point across. For instance, **Proverbs 27:23-24** says, *"Know well the condition of your flocks, and give attention to your herds, for riches do not last forever; and does a crown endure to all generations?"* Notice how both the advice and the reason for the advice are given twice? The repetition simply helps get the point across.

A few chapters in Proverbs carry a longer message. Proverbs 5-7 include lengthy warnings from a father to his son against adultery. Proverbs 31 is the classic chapter on how to be a godly woman. On that note, another word of wisdom is in order. Some teaching that I have heard about Proverbs 31 has been too literal with what is, again, general advice. For that reason, I've written the following section, which should help you understand how to interpret this chapter of Proverbs.

The Proverbs 31 Woman

Go ahead and read Proverbs 31 right now to familiarize your-self with the context. Then come back and tackle this section. Some Bible teachers assert that modern Christian women are supposed to literally imitate the actions of the woman described in **Proverbs 31:10-31.** They claim that to be a "Proverbs 31 woman," a Christian woman must get up before dawn because along with other things in the chapter, verse 15 says, *"She rises while it is yet night and provides food for her household and portions for her maidens."*

This literal view has even led some teachers to claim things like, "A Christian woman must also help bring in financial income for her family" because verse 16 says, "*She goes to inspect a field and buys it; with her earnings she plants a vineyard.*"

The people who make this argument claim that each and every action of the woman listed in Proverbs 31 has a literal action or principle directly transferable to today's Christian woman. While we as evangelical Christians believe in a literal interpretation of the Bible, a literal interpretation of Proverbs 31 does not hold up under closer examination.

The first clue that this isn't the correct way to interpret this passage is that the passage itself is found in the book of Proverbs. As you have learned, the Proverbs are not specific promises that God is accountable to perform for his people, but general wisdom that, if followed, usually leads to good results. An example is **Proverbs 28:23**: "*Whoever rebukes a man will afterward find more favor than he who flatters with his tongue.*" Does this mean that every time you or I rebuke someone, the person will respond positively? Of course not; there are always exceptions to the rule. This proverb presents the principle that correcting someone, even though it's difficult to do, is the better thing to do in the long run. It's not a specific promise or literal guideline for every situation.

This is true of all the proverbs and especially Proverbs 31. It gives general principles for women to follow. It's not a magical formula that guarantees success, and it is not meant to be followed literally.

Another reason that Proverbs 31 is not to be taken literally is that most women of that time and culture, as in every time period and culture, were not as well off financially as the woman in this Proverb. Paying attention to the historical context in this Proverb yields important clues. For instance, the woman portrayed in this Proverb has servants. She has enough money of her own to buy a field, clothing of fine linen and purple. Her husband is a leader in their community. All of these facts make it clear that this woman was wealthy. The modern equivalent is a well-to-do woman who employs household help, runs her own business or perhaps is a physician, and whose husband is a respected official in the community.

Most women throughout history have never had the advantages that the Proverbs 31 woman had. Does that mean God is upset or disappointed that most women cannot fulfill these expectations because they don't have the financial means to do so? Of course not.

In the Old Covenant with Israel, part of God's blessing to the Israeli people was financial security if they served him faithfully. God's promise to us in Jesus is not the same. His covenant with us promises spiritual riches and security in eternity. That does not mean that we can't glean anything good from Proverbs 31. We need to draw out the timeless principles rather than specific actions. For example, we see the benefits of hard work vs. laziness in verses 13-19.

One last but important clue that Proverbs 31 is to be taken symbolically rather than literally is this: **Proverbs 31:10-31** is an acrostic poem that was meant for Hebrew children to memorize. Each verse begins with the next letter in the Hebrew alphabet, much like this:

A – A godly woman is the glory of her household,
B – Because she never ceases to praise God for her daily bread,
C – Coming from the store with the best bargains,
D – Delivering to her family all good things.

For us, the acrostic nature of the poem was lost in the translation to English. The underlying meaning of the poem is still the same. Its purpose is still to give a general sketch, an outline, of what a godly woman can be to her family.

In summary, as we draw out principles from this passage, we must be careful never to *over apply* these verses to mean something they do not. The entire book of Proverbs is part of the Old Testament "wisdom" literature, all of which give general guidelines that, if followed, usually lead to blessing. Turning Proverbs 31 into a literal guideline that it was never intended to be puts a heavy burden on Christian women that God never intended.

Philosophy for the Ages: Job & Ecclesiastes

Job and Ecclesiastes are in some ways similar to Proverbs, but their format is different than Proverbs. In each, the main argument consists of an extended conversation that leads to a grand point at the end. I can guarantee, though, that the hard work is worth the pearl of wisdom you will obtain if you stick with it! Reading these books can be likened to meeting good friends at Starbucks every week to discuss questions of deep significance. The great questions of life take time to answer. People's beliefs change slowly, over time. It's a process of thought, analysis and discussion.

Most people usually don't evaluate their beliefs and values unless they are forced to. The books of Job and Ecclesiastes were written by two men that had their values and life circumstances challenged by God. Therefore, it's all the more important to understand the context of Job and Ecclesiastes. Knowing the context helps the reader discover that these books were not written from an ivory tower, but through the pen of suffering and life experience by people who knew great hardship and pain.

Ecclesiastes

Most conservative scholars believe that King Solomon wrote Ecclesiastes. The Scriptures declare that he was the wisest man who ever lived **I Kings 4:30-32**. He also possessed great wealth. The Bible proclaims that during his reign, silver lost value in the Israeli monetary system because it was so common in Jerusalem **I Kings 10:26-28, II Chronicles 9:27**. The biblical accounts of his wealth are truly stunning. Bill Gates and Warren Buffett had nothing on King Solomon!

Although Solomon was a wise and just king, later on in life he allowed himself to be corrupted by his many wives, who turned his heart away from God. He even allowed these wives to set up idols to their own gods **I Kings 11:3-7**. It appears that after this period, at the end of his life, Solomon wrote the book of Ecclesiastes. Solomon was a man who had every opportunity available to man. His wealth was limitless, his power untouchable and his mental abilities unmatched. With this background in mind, we come to the book of Ecclesiastes.

Ecclesiastes takes twelve chapters to come to its point. I don't encourage you to spend a lot of time "looking for what God is saying to you" in chapter 2. It is not a self-contained unit of text, but part of a larger framework in which the author, Solomon, goes back and forth in his mind about the meaning of life and human existence. It isn't until the end of the book that the author writes, "Fear God and keep his commandments, for this is the whole duty of man" **Ecclesiastes 12:13**. If you tried to glean God's message to you from an earlier portion of the book, you could be misled or confused if you stopped at **Ecclesiastes 6:1-4,** for instance, which portrays a VERY despondent view of life.

Therefore, it is imperative when reading Job or Ecclesiastes to remember that the point of each book is not revealed until the end. The conversations that take place throughout each book guide the reader toward the right point of view in the end, but are not intended to be taken as separate pieces.

Solomon wants to make sure the reader understands that he literally tried EVERYTHING to make himself happy. He denied himself nothing, but in the end, he comes back to the perspective that the only justifiable way to live is to fear God and do what he says. This is wisdom from a man who had everything at his disposal and took many paths in life.

Job

The book of Job is a very early account of the struggle between good and evil. It's a long book by Biblical standards with forty-two chapters. Biblical scholars believe Job lived at or around the same time as Abraham (see his story in the book of Genesis) who lived around 2000 to 1800 BC. The book of Job, then, is almost 4,000 years old. Its main theme is "Why do bad things happen to good people?" People still ask that question today, don't they?

Job is a righteous man who is used as a player in a cosmic challenge between God and Satan. Satan believes that Job worships God only because God has blessed him so much. So, added to the main theme, "Why do bad things happen to good people?" is an added element: "Will a righteous man turn his back on God in bad times?" In this situation, God allows Satan to take away everything that Job owns or holds dear. After this series of unfortunate events happens to Job, the rest of the story is a many-layered conversation between Job, his three best friends, one stranger, and finally, at the end, God himself.

This conversation focused ONLY on one topic: *Why did this happen to Job?* His friends give various responses, all of which implicate Job in some form. Job continues to defend his innocence. At the end of the book, God shows up and humbles everybody, including Job. He doesn't give the answers that everybody wants to hear. God shows himself to be majestic and glorious through this process.

In the final scene of the book, God again blesses Job with more wealth than he possessed at the beginning. God shows his favor toward his servant Job, but he doesn't answer the questions that have been asked of him. As you read Job, you'll notice that God doesn't neatly tie up the loose ends as we like. This is an important point, showing the difference between the Bible and other ancient or modern books on philosophy.

The traditional goal of philosophy is knowing or arriving at answers to life's big questions. The goal of the Bible, on the other hand, is worshiping and knowing God. Therefore, although the book of Job is much like other ancient writings in that it retells a conversation between a man and his friends, all seeking answers, it is different in that the final act of the book is one where God gets the glory and men are humbled.

Job, as with the other wisdom literature, gives us brief glimpses into some of the grand schemes of God. **Job 19:25-26** is an incredible passage about Job's hope in the resurrection! *"For I know that my Redeemer lives, and at the last he will stand upon the earth. And after my skin has been thus destroyed, yet in my flesh I shall see God."*

Job 38-42 relates a prolonged speech from the Lord about creation. Those chapters present God as a grand architect who designed the universe and all the creatures on the earth. Even as God deals with Job and his friends, we receive a glimpse into his divine majesty and glory. God himself describes the creatures that he has made. It is awesome to listen to the Creator talk about his creation.

I hope this chapter has been helpful as you seek to mine the wisdom available to us in Scripture through these ancient books. Whether it's short, four-line poetry in Proverbs or the great questions of life in Job and Ecclesiastes, the wisdom literature of the Bible is philosophy at its greatest: thinking about God, fearing him, serving him and being obedient to him.

Chapter 6

Poetry
Psalms, Song of Solomon

W hen I write an e-mail to a co-worker in ministry, it usually contains such things as times and dates, projects and deadlines, and general encouragements. On the other hand, when I write a letter to my wife about how much I love her, suddenly I begin to write about the moon, the stars, flowers, a gentle breeze and the sea.

Why does this happen? It's because I have one language for work and another language for love. By "language" I mean that I use different styles of writing depending on my purpose. In this chapter we'll look at God's use of poetry in the Old Testament.

The poetry of the Old Testament can be taken in much the same way as a reader understands the poetry of today. Poetry has a point to relay, but almost never in absolutely literal terms. Webster's Dictionary defines poetry as *"writing... chosen and arranged to create a specific emotional response through meaning, sound, and rhythm."* Simply put, it relays experience or information via feelings rather than just literal description. Don't misunderstand and think that this means poetic writing isn't truthful. Poetry can transmit great truth, but it does so in a way that captures the reader's imagination.

The longest book of the Bible, the Psalms, is a collection of poems and songs. There are different kinds of Psalms, written for different reasons. I've compiled some of the more useful information available to help you learn how to read and understand the Psalms.[1]

Before we get to the specific kinds of songs and poems found in the Psalms, though, let's review. If you try to interpret some of the Psalms literally, you're going to get into trouble. While I say my wife has eyes that sparkle like diamonds, the local jeweler might disagree (but if he does, he's wrong!). I used poetic language to describe my wife's beautiful eyes.

I must note here that when we use metaphorical terms to describe God, our language can never measure up because God's magnificence rises so far beyond what we are able to express. When the author of a Psalm describes God as a shield to those who trust in him, **Psalm 118:9**, it actually means God is *better* than a shield. Unlike human comparisons, which sometimes fall short, God always *exceeds* the thing he is being compared to. The Psalms liken God to a shield, a fortress, a strong tower, a rock, a hiding place, a shepherd, a judge, a king and a warrior. In truth, he is ALL those things, and also much more than our finite minds can imagine.

So, why do we call this book of the Bible the Psalms? In Greek the word "psalmos," means "to sing" from which we derive the word "Psalms." The original Hebrew title of the book was "tahaleem," which means "praises." I prefer that title, but as a pastor, if I told my congregation to open up their Bibles to the book of Tahaleem, they would think I am crazy! English language Bibles got the title from the Greek translation of the Old Testament, which is called the Septuagint.

The Psalms were part of the corporate worship of Israel. When the people gathered in the Temple, they recited or sang Psalms together. They sang certain songs or recited particular psalms when celebrating special feasts or holidays, just as we sing "Silent Night" at Christmas and "Christ the Lord Is Risen Today" on Easter. People wrote new Psalms in response to God's blessing or deliverance of the nation.

The Psalms are prayers, songs and poems. Expressions like "The trees of the field will clap their hands" are not meant to be taken as universal (true for everybody) or literal statements. The Psalms relay deep truth about the human heart and the universe itself in poetic ways. A little understanding of Hebrew poetry will enhance your love of the Psalms.

Remember: the author of a Psalm expresses himself creatively and passionately rather than logically.

The Psalms use a literary device called "parallelism." Parallelism is just a five-star word that means repeating something in different ways. Once you get the feel for it, the Psalms have more meaning for you. The writers use different kinds of parallelism in the Psalms. I will guide you through the major sections so that you understand and appreciate what the Psalms are saying.

Who wrote the Psalms? They are unique in Scripture because they have so many different authors. The most well-known author is King David, but he only wrote about half of the Psalms. Following are the authors we know (revealed in Scripture).

David wrote seventy-three (roughly half of them).

Solomon wrote two (Psalms 72 and 127).

Moses wrote Psalm 90.

The family of Asaph wrote eleven (Psalms 50 and 73-83).

The sons of Korah wrote eleven (Psalms 42, 44-49, 84-85, 87-88).

Heman wrote one (Psalm 88).

Ethan the Ezrahite wrote one (Psalm 89).

The other Psalms were written by unnamed Israelites.

The Psalms are divided into 5 books.

Book I: Psalms 1-41
Book II: Psalms 42-72
Book III: Psalms 73-89
Book IV: Psalms 90-106
Book V: Psalms 107-150

Who divided them that way? The ancient Israelites did. Why? We don't know. (Lots of good information here, huh?)

The Psalms can also be categorized by topic or purpose as follows:

Psalms of Lament – Help Me, God!

These comprise the biggest category of Psalms. This is a personal or a national cry for help to God based on the situation of the writer or the nation as a whole. Psalms of personal lament include: 3-7, 13, 17, 22, 25-28, 31, 35, 39, 42-43, 51, 54-57, 59, 61-64, 70-71, 77, 86, 88, 102, 120, 130, 140-143. The Psalms of national lament are Psalms 44, 74, 79-80, 83, 85, 90, 94, and 137.

The Psalms of lament remind us intensely that life is hard. Sometimes we get ourselves into bad situations and cry out for help to God. Sometimes people persecute us for no good reason and we cry out for relief from their attacks. Either way, Psalms of lament are full of emotion and pain. These Psalms could also be titled, "The Psalms of Pain." Personally, I'm really glad these Psalms are a part of Scripture. Countless times in my life I have cried out to God from these Psalms of lament. These Psalms have given comfort to the suffering for thousands of years. They aren't the best thing to read when you're full of joy and it's your birthday, but when life is tough, these are the Psalms to read. Another great thing about these Psalms is that the perspective always comes around to God. Even in the most desperate situations, at the end of most of these Psalms you find the author returning to his hope and peace in God.

Psalms of Praise and Thanksgiving – Thank You, Lord!

These are also classified as **individual** and **group** Psalms. We find individuals praising God in Psalms 8, 18, 30, 32-34, 40, 66, 75, 81, 92, 103-104, 106, 108, 111-113, 116, 118, 135, 138, 145-150. The group praise Psalms are 65, 67, 107, 114, 117, 124, and 136.

All these Psalms are prayers and songs of thanksgiving. These are your prayers when life is good or the Lord has just come through in a big way. I remember one night I was singing praise songs and psalms in my head until I went to sleep. I was young and working in ministry, trying to be a good husband and father of three children while going to school at the same time. Ministry wasn't paying very much, and I was thinking about returning to another job I'd had before becoming an assistant pastor. Then I got a phone call from someone in the church who told me that he had come into some money and felt that he was supposed to help us. He wanted to pay our rent for the year! Twelve months of no rent payment. Do you think I was happy? Do you think I was singing praise to the Lord Most High? As soon as my wife walked in from the grocery store she said she wanted to tell me something. I said, "Wait! Whatever you have to tell me right now is not as important as what I have to tell you!" But she didn't believe me and proceeded to tell me what she had to say. Only after that did I get to tell her about how God had just miraculously provided for us. Then my individual praise psalm turned into a group praise psalm as my wife and I jumped for joy all over the house for about two hours. That's the kind of jubilant emotion the praise and thanksgiving psalms express.

Psalms of Zion – Jerusalem the Beautiful

These Psalms focus on **Jerusalem** and the **Temple**. They are 46, 48, 76, 84, 87, 122, and 137.

It's important for us to remember that the city of Jerusalem, and specifically the Temple, was extremely important to the Jews. Jerusalem was called "The city of the great King." The King referred not to a man, but to God. The Jews saw Jerusalem as the center of the world. Inside Jerusalem was God's Holy Temple where he manifested his physical presence to Solomon and the Israelites, **I Kings 8:10-11**. The Israelites talked about Jerusalem and the Temple the way we talk of heaven. David was likely referring to the Temple when he wrote in **Psalm 27:4,** *"One thing have I asked of the Lord, that will I seek after: that I may dwell in the house of the Lord all the days of my life, to gaze upon the beauty of the Lord and to inquire in his temple."* When we Christians read that poem, we think of God's heavenly dwelling place. That's completely acceptable because God's presence does not reside in a Temple made by man. Although

David may have been thinking of the Temple, we see this Psalm's ultimate fulfillment in the heavenly court of God.

Royal Psalms – God Save the King

Most of these Psalms refer to God's "Anointed King," or Messiah. They are 2, 18, 20-21, 45, 72, 89, 101, 110, 132, 144.

As Jerusalem and the Temple were the most significant structures to the Jews, the most important person was the king. This is a similar characteristic to many ancient cultures, but the Jews made one key distinction: they believed that one day, through the family line of King David, God would send a powerful Messiah and deliverer. Therefore, the Psalms include many songs and poems about that future king as well as the present king and his family line. We see in these Psalms powerful imagery about the Messiah, Jesus.

Wisdom Psalms – Listen to This

The wisdom Psalms function more like proverbs than poetry. Their aim is to teach the reader something. They are Psalms 1, 37, 49, 73, 112, 127-128, and 133.

Many of these Psalms read as long conversations, like Proverbs 5 or 31. They teach wisdom through imaginary dialogue or as if the author is talking to himself. Like the other wisdom literature we studied, these Psalms take a few verses to get the proper perspective. These Psalms sometimes begin with an accusation of God or a bitter cry about how life is unfair. Only through the process of digging out his emotions and getting real with God does the author come to God's viewpoint. The author learns something in these Psalms and relays it to the reader.

Trust Psalms – Don't Go Off the Edge!

While similar to praise and thanksgiving, a specific theme of trust in God runs through Psalms 11, 16, 23, 62, 91, 121, 125, and 131. These Psalms exhort the reader to "wait on the Lord" or to "trust in the Lord." They also admonish the reader to understand that unless the Lord initiates a work, it is useless to attempt it. These Psalms are good to remember when we're proud of our own accomplishments.

One Psalm in this category in particular provides great comfort to believers. As a pastor, I have sat by the bedsides of a fair number of seriously ill people, some of them dying. Over and over, people have asked me to read Psalm 23 to them. Even people who don't seem to be very spiritual are comforted by it. Mature Christians long to hear it when they are suffering. Psalm 23 embodies the perfect expression of dependence on God and God's gentle care of his people. It is the most beautiful poem in the world. I am not a professor of literature, but I can make that claim because I have seen the comfort it can give to dying people. Why is it so powerful? Perhaps because it so beautifully displays our relationship to God and our dependence on him, which those who suffer know better than anyone.

The Psalms are full of the shouts of triumph and the groans of bitter agony of God's people. In short, they capture life through poetic expression. They accurately relate the tremendous ups and downs of life.

My own personal belief is that Christians should always read the Psalms as part of their daily Bible reading. With 150 of them, if you read one every day, it will take almost a half of a year to read through them. I suggest that you even read them right before you begin your prayers. Often, when I am distracted or when I don't think I have the right frame of mind to begin my prayers, reading a Psalm centers my mind upon the awesome and incredible God that I serve. Then I am able to enter into God's presence more acutely aware of who he is and what he has done for me.

The Song of Solomon or Song of Songs

The Song of Solomon is so graphic in its description of love between a man and his wife that for many years the church sought to interpret it solely as an allegory of love between Christ and the church. More recently, however, scholars have come to understand its importance as a love poem between a man and a woman. If God created men and women to be married to one another, it is no surprise that he also saw fit to offer us one book of the Bible dedicated to the joy of physical attraction and love in marriage.

The book is a play with three actors: the husband, the wife, and the people looking on. In most translations these observers are titled "friends" or "others." In a series of songs, the action moves from the man to the woman to the reactions of the onlookers. The man confesses his love for the woman and she for him. Back and forth it goes as they rejoice and consummate their relationship in marriage.

The Song of Solomon may not be a book to study over and over for personal devotions like the book of Proverbs, but it's a wonderful example of God's joy in creating a man and a woman to love one another and the delight that godly people can enjoy in following God's plan for them.

This book also contains poetic verses that can be rightly applied to both a godly husband and to Jesus as our king and Lord: *"He brought me to the banqueting house, and his banner over me was love"* **Song of Solomon 2:4**. Since the New Testament calls the Church the bride of Christ in **II Corinthians 11:2**, the metaphor of God as the husband and the Church as the wife makes sense. We must keep in mind, however, that the main context of the book is that of romantic love between a human husband and wife, which culminates in their wedding night together.

As you become familiar with biblical poetry, remember that it is an emotional expression of the heart toward God. Sometimes it's done with passionate abandon, and sometimes in great wisdom. Biblical truth isn't just dry doctrine spelled out in do's and don'ts. It conveys a loving relationship with the God of the universe that is deeply moving and authentic in the innermost parts of our souls. It's fitting that it finds expression in these wonderful poetic books of Scripture.

Chapter 7

Old Testament Prophecy
Isaiah – Malachi

Nelson's *New Illustrated Bible Dictionary* defines prophecy as: "Predictions about the future and the end time; special messages from God, often uttered through a human spokesperson."[2] To that definition I would add, "Giving messages that people really need to hear."

Biblical prophecy and biblical prophets have always had dual roles; they told people both present and future truth. They were truth tellers more than fortune tellers. They did give messages about the future, but they also held people accountable to what they were supposed to be doing in the here and now.

In the Old Testament, the Law showed how God wanted people to live. The prophets served as the spiritual police force, encouraging and convicting the nation to turn back to the things that God wanted from them. In this way, the Old Testament prophets were like your pesky kid sister who's always telling you what you're doing wrong. I don't know one person who actually likes it when someone tells them what they're doing wrong. Often, the people of Israel treated the prophets exactly like a kid sister; they ignored them. If the prophets continued talking, the people threatened them with violence.

Since Israel was governed by a divine law from God, he wanted more than just grudging acceptance or trying to get by with following as little of the law as possible. He longed for people to conform with their whole hearts to the pattern of life that he laid down for them.

The main message of the prophets was "live right with God and man." Over and over in the prophetic sections of Scripture you find a prophet rebuking a person, official or nation because of their injustice toward others, their pride, or their uncaring attitude. This is perhaps the most helpful portion of the books of prophecy. Even if I don't know how and when a certain prophecy was fulfilled, I still learn what is in God's heart and the obedience he desires from his people.

For instance, in **Micah 2:2-3**, God pronounces judgment on the wicked land owners of Judah. He says: *"They covet fields and seize them, and houses, and take them away; they oppress a man and his house, a man and his inheritance. Therefore thus says the Lord: behold, against this family I am devising disaster, from which you cannot remove your necks."* The message is: "You take land from the poor and cause disaster to come upon them. Because you do that, I will bring disaster upon you." We can learn a lot from sections like this one. Besides the general principle, "Don't steal from poor people because it's wrong," we learn that God sees everything that is done and he knows the motives of all people. No one committing unjust and evil deeds escapes the hand of God. The prophets offer these reminders over and over.

What We Know (and Don't Know) About Fulfillment of Prophecy

Throughout the history of the Church, Christians have disagreed about the nature of certain prophecies in the Bible: whether they refer to the end times, whether they have already been fulfilled, or whether it is a mix of both, sort of a double fulfillment of Scripture. Christians want to know whether or not Old Testament prophecies apply to them. It's just like when I file my income tax return every year; my basic question each time is "Do I owe more or do I not owe more?"

A few factors make interpreting prophecy difficult at times. The first is that although God may have told an Old Testament prophet to proclaim a message about the future, we don't always have the historical record of how the prophecy came to pass later on. That doesn't mean that the prophecy wasn't fulfilled. It tells us that the message God wanted us to have was the warning to a certain country or individual.

Many times the Bible includes both the prediction and its fulfillment. Other times Scripture uses symbols in a prediction and then interprets those symbols for us. A case in point is **Daniel 8:1-27**. Verses 1-15 describe the vision that Daniel had. Verses 16-27 explain what the vision is about. Daniel saw a vision of a ram and a male goat. The text gives some clues about who is portrayed in the vision, but it's not completely clear until you get to verses 20-21, which read, *"As for the ram that you saw with the two horns, these are the kings of Media and Persia. And the goat is the king of Greece."*

So having the vision or prophecy explained by Scripture itself (there's that analogy of Scripture working!) is a great help. Then you're able to connect the dots and the details of the vision together with other prophecies in a more intelligent way because the main plot has been communicated.

Now, all prophecy is not this difficult to interpret. In many prophetic passages, God tells the prophet, "Concerning Egypt and Pharaoh, say this…" Needless to say, you know that particular prophecy is about Egypt.

Those Old Testament Prophets Did Some Strange Things

Old Testament prophets had to do weird stuff. Once God told a prophet to bury a nice garment by the riverside and dig it up later. One was called to lie down on his right side for a certain number of days. Once a prophet had to gather all his luggage, go to the city wall and dig a hole through the wall at a place where a lot of people could see him. One prophet repeatedly called down fire from heaven to destroy the soldiers who had come to arrest him. There seems to be no end to the strange things that God commanded these men to do.

Although the nation of Israel worshiped God, it was no different than many other Middle Eastern nations in that the king had all the power. When God called the prophets to do strange things or to perform miracles, those actions sent a message to the king that God was still in control. The miracles were a sign that although the king had an army, *God's power was the source of their success.*

The strange actions that the prophets performed were a sign of how far God was willing to go to get the nation to pay attention. Have you ever had a class in school where the teacher did something different or unusual to grab the class' attention? God's commanding the prophets to do strange things is similar to that. He did everything he could to get their attention. If they still refused to listen to him, then they deserved their punishment.

The Three Kinds of Prophecies in the Bible

In learning to interpret prophecy, it's safe to say that most Bible scholars agree that the Bible contains three kinds of prophecies:

A) General prophecies about the future
B) Prophecies about the Messiah
C) Prophecies about the end times/end of the world

Knowing these will help you as you study God's Word on your own. Before we delve into the three kinds of prophecies, however, I need to make two disclaimers: Interpreting prophecy is not always clear cut. Two concepts, one known as "double fulfillment" and the other, "the day of the Lord", mix readers up. Both of these ideas come up fairly regularly. I'll give you examples of these concepts before I explain the general kinds of prophecy found in the Bible.

Double Fulfillment

Isaiah 7:10-16 – *[10] Not long after this, the LORD sent this message to King Ahaz: [11] "Ask me for a sign, Ahaz, to prove that I will crush your enemies as I have promised. Ask for anything you like, and make it as difficult as you want." [12] But the king refused. "No," he said, "I wouldn't test the LORD like that." [13] Then Isaiah said, "Listen well, you royal* *family of David! You aren't satisfied to exhaust my patience. You exhaust the patience of God as well! [14] All right then, the Lord himself will choose the sign. Look! <u>The virgin</u> [Hebrew: "almah," young woman of marriageable age] <u>will conceive a child!</u> She will give birth to a son and will call him Immanuel — 'God is with us' [15] By the time this child is old enough to eat curds and honey, he will know enough to choose what is right and reject what is wrong. [16] But before he knows right from wrong, the two kings you fear so much—the kings of Israel and Aram—will both be dead."* (NLT, Hebrew translation mine.)

In this section of Scripture, God is speaking through Isaiah the prophet to Judah's King Ahaz, telling him to ask for a sign that God's Word to him would prove true. Ahaz will not ask for a sign, so God gives him one anyway: "The virgin will be with child."

God goes on to tell Ahaz that by the time the child is old enough to choose right from wrong, the two kings whom Ahaz fears, the kings of Israel and Aram, will both be dead. Therefore, because this prophecy is directed at Ahaz and a sign is given to Ahaz, it's safe to say that he will be alive to see it happen. A few years after this sign was given, a young woman gave birth to a child and before he was old enough to know right from wrong, the kings of Israel and Aram were dead. Ahaz was probably alive to see this prophecy fulfilled.

Christians, however, are familiar with this prophecy for a completely different reason. This Scripture is the one that predicts the virgin birth of Jesus Christ to Mary. That is the second fulfillment of the Scripture.

You may have noticed, in the passage from Isaiah quoted above, I added the Hebrew word for virgin, "almah," used in that passage. It means a young woman of marriageable age. It assumes the woman is a virgin because any proper young Hebrew woman of marriageable age would have remained a virgin until her wedding day. Therefore, the Hebrew word "almah" can be correctly translated as either "young woman" or "virgin." When the Savior is to be born in Israel hundreds of years later, an angel visits Joseph, Mary's fiancé, telling him:

"Joseph, son of David, do not fear to take Mary as your wife, for that which is conceived in her is from the Holy Spirit. She will bear a son, and you shall call his name Jesus, for he will save his people from their sins." All this took place to fulfill what the Lord had spoken by the prophet: "Behold, the virgin shall conceive and bear a son, and they shall call his name Immanuel" **Matthew 1:20a-23**

In Matthew, Mary is engaged to Joseph; she is a virgin. She conceives a child through the Holy Spirit and that fulfills the prophecy from way back in Isaiah's time. Was the prophecy fulfilled the first time when the kings of Israel and Aram died? Yes. Was it fulfilled a second time when Jesus was born of a virgin woman? Yes. This prophecy has a double fulfillment.

I've given you an example of double fulfillment because often, New Testament authors point out a fulfillment of prophecy that doesn't fit what you or I would consider the natural fulfillment of an Old Testament prophecy. Don't let this throw you off. When the Holy Spirit works through the authors of Scripture to indicate a second fulfillment, he's displaying God's power to orchestrate human events in such a way that one prophecy can be fulfilled in two different ways or more than once.

Did You Know?

> **Many important prophecies in the Old Testament have more than one fulfillment.**

The Day of the Lord

When my kids were little, we had a tradition on family birthdays. After the birthday person went to bed the night before their birthday, the rest of my family stayed up and decorated the house with paper streamers. We placed special cards, candy and presents at that person's place at the table. The next day, the birthday person got to choose what the whole family ate for breakfast, lunch and dinner. We did what that person wanted to do on "their day." Since it was their birthday, they got to choose everything that happened.

The day of the Lord is a little like this. It's going to be a day when he chooses everything that happens in a very unique and very specific way. Theologically, the day of the Lord means the same thing as the Second Coming of Jesus Christ.

Both the Old and New Testaments contain many references to "the day of the Lord." The apostle Peter gives some details about it in **II Peter 3:10** and the prophet Obadiah talks about it in **Obadiah 1:15:** *"For the day of the Lord is near upon all the nations."*

References to this day abound in the Old Testament prophetic books. As a general rule, a basic definition of the day of the Lord is "The time when God ends world history and judges the earth." The reason I defined it as "time" instead of "day" is because a few prophecies indicate that "the day of the Lord" refers not just to the actual day when he will come back but to the period of time when God will take over the earth.

The day of the Lord also refers to the events of the end times that precede his Second Coming. The plagues that God will send on the unbelieving world in advance of his return are events involved in the day of the Lord.

This doesn't mean that there isn't an actual "day" on which Jesus will come back; there most certainly will be. What I said before still stands: if it takes weeks or months to usher in the events preceding the time of the Lord's return, you can safely include all those events as part of "the day of the Lord."

The day of the Lord can be seen as a wonderful thing *or* an awful thing. It's a wonderful thing because God will finally do away with all evil, but in doing so, he will inflict a lot of pain on the world. He will judge and purge the evil in the world when he comes. An example of this is found in **Micah 1:1-7**. Micah foretells the judgment and exile of Judah and Jerusalem, but we can detect overtones of the day of the Lord in the passage as well. It's not a happy passage. Since wicked people will suffer greatly on the day of the Lord, it will be a terrible day in that respect. God loves all people and desires that everybody be saved. God does not delight in inflicting punishment on the wicked. He would rather have them turn from their wickedness.

The Day of the Lord Seen in Double Fulfillment Prophecies

Now that you have learned these two concepts, it's time to put them together. Since the events of the day of the Lord are so terrible, and since God wants everyone to avoid the pain, he began warning of his final judgment way back in Old Testament times through double fulfillment prophecies.

The best way someone explained it to me was this: Pretend you're looking at a house on a nearby hill, and behind the hill is a HUGE mountain rising into the clouds. You can clearly see the house on the hill and its details, but almost overshadowing the hill in your sight and imagination is the mountain behind it. The hill and mountain represent double fulfillment prophecies concerning Israel in the Old Testament and the end times. The house on the hill is the first fulfillment and the mountain is the final or second fulfillment

The Lord directed prophets to preach against the wickedness of the people of Israel, but he also allowed the prophets to see beyond the immediate wickedness of the people of Israel to the ultimate wickedness that will bring about the end of the world as we know it. The house on the hill in our analogy is the immediate and local concern. The mountain is the wickedness in the end times that brings about the day of the Lord.

The House on the Hill = **The immediate and local concern**
The Mountain = **the ultimate or bigger concern,
such as the day of the Lord.**

In the short book of Joel, the Lord sent a plague of locusts because of the people's wickedness. The Lord also used the plague to show Joel the ultimate destruction that would come about in the great and terrible day of the Lord. When reading prophecy, you will often see God switch gears like this through a prophet. Don't let it confuse you; just recognize that God is referring to both local and worldwide prophecy.

Keeping in mind the concepts of double fulfillment and the day of the Lord prophecies, let's proceed to the three specific kinds of prophecy found in the prophetical books.

General Prophecies About the Future

The Old Testament is full of prophecies about the future, most of which have been fulfilled. Many of the prophecies in the Old Testament pertained to the people of Israel and their national conduct.

Many prophets warned the Hebrews not to disobey God. When they did, the punishment for their disobedience was exile from their land. The Israelites ignored the warnings from the prophets and were taken as captives to Assyria and Babylon before 500 AD. So those prophecies have come to pass.

Similarly, God also blessed or cursed neighboring nations depending on their conduct toward the Israelites. **Jeremiah 46-51** announces the punishments that God has planned for the nations of Egypt, Philistia, Moab, Ammon, Edom, Elam and Babylon. All those prophecies have been fulfilled. The nation of the Philistines doesn't even exist any more, so we know their portion of prophecy has been fulfilled!

Before you toss aside this information as useless to you, consider this: what if God gave specific messages to prophets today for the countries of Canada, the United States, Mexico, China, England, or even the states of California or New York. Most of us would be eager to find out what God would say to those countries or states! It's fascinating to read some of the Old Testament prophecies to determine the kinds of issues the countries and kingdoms of those times dealt with.

Included in general prophecies about the future are "if...then" prophecies. This kind of prophecy is spelled out explicitly in **Jeremiah 18:5-10**.

*5 Then the L*ORD *gave me this message: 6 "O Israel, can I not do to you as this potter has done to his clay? As the clay is in the potter's hand, so are you in my hand. 7 **If** I announce that a certain nation or kingdom is to be uprooted, torn down, and destroyed, 8 but **then** that nation renounces its evil ways, I will not destroy it as I had planned. 9 And **if** I announce that I will plant and build up a certain nation or kingdom, 10 but **then** that nation turns to evil and refuses to obey me, I will not bless it as I said I would. (NLT)*

You will also find "if … then" prophecies and fulfillments in Deuteronomy 28 and Ezekiel 3 and 33.

The book of Jonah relates an "if … then" prophecy in specific detail. The gist of it is this: If God issues a prophetic warning to a people or nation because they are wicked and they change their ways, then God will relent and not bring on them the disaster that he warned them about. But if they do not, then he will fulfill all that he promised against them.

This if…then concept is helpful to know because we tend to think of God's words as set in stone at all times. Since God is so intelligent and powerful that he knows what will happen based on the choices that people make, he does urge people to turn from their wicked ways, and warns them what will happen if they don't.

Some people conclude from such passages that God is limited in his power. They believe that God doesn't actually know the future. It's times like these when the analogy of Scripture helps us yet again. The Bible declares openly and specifically that God knows everything: *"remember the former things of old; for I am God, and there is no other; I am God, and there is none like me, declaring the end from the beginning and from ancient times things not yet done, saying, 'My counsel shall stand, and I will accomplish all my purpose,'"* **Isaiah 46:9-10**.

Instead of looking at the "if…then" passages and thinking that they limit God, we should see instead how graciously God deals with us. He is the Lord of time and space, and he chooses to give us the chance to repent. If we do, he will change his disposition and look favorably on us. What an incredible God we serve!

Prophecies About the Messiah

I've heard that more than three hundred separate prophecies in the Old Testament concerning the Messiah were fulfilled by Jesus when he lived among us — from his place of birth to the type of ministry he would perform to his suffering and resurrection.

Jesus is so central to the Bible, even in the Old Testament, that I felt I needed to address messianic prophecies in this chapter. Some of the more well-known are Isaiah 9 and 53, and Psalm 22. As a Christian, I find great joy in reading these prophecies.

These writings give me insight into the character and ministry of Christ that I might never have had if they hadn't been written. For instance, **Isaiah 53:2-3** says, *"he had no form or majesty that we should look at him, and no beauty that we should desire him. He was despised and rejected by men; a man of sorrows, and acquainted with grief."* The Gospels give no description of the physical appearance of Jesus. But from Isaiah's prophecy I get the picture that Jesus wasn't the most handsome of men. Now, we shouldn't be too concerned with exactly what Jesus looked like, because in the end it doesn't matter. Nevertheless, it is incredible to know that when God came down and lived with us humans, he took on the "form of a servant" as Philippians 2 says, and chose to inhabit a body that looked like an average person's; He wasn't physically beautiful.

Another reason it is important to study the Old Testament prophecies about Jesus is that the early Church emphatically declared that Jesus fulfilled the Scriptures as the Jewish Messiah. In the book of Acts, when the gospel spread, it spread by the Christians going into the Jewish synagogues, *[1]Now when they had passed through Amphipolis and Apollonia, they came to Thessalonica, where there was a synagogue of the Jews. [2]And Paul went in, as was his custom, and on three Sabbath days he reasoned with them from the Scriptures, [3]explaining and proving that it was necessary for the Christ to suffer and to rise from the dead, and saying, 'This Jesus, whom I proclaim to you, is the Christ'"* **Acts 17:1-3**.

At the time, the only Scriptures that Jews and early Christians agreed were from God were what we now know as the Old Testament. Early Church leaders such as Peter, John, Stephen, Paul, Apollos,

Barnabas, Silas, Aquila and Priscilla were all well-versed in the Old Testament passages that proved that Jesus was the Christ.

It is important that Christians be able to show unbelievers who Jesus is and where he came from. The place to start is the Old Testament prophecies about him. In fact, **Psalm 22** paints such a clear picture of the crucifixion of Jesus that when I have read it to people they have expressed shock and disbelief that a passage so parallel to the crucifixion account exists in the Psalms. King David wrote this Psalm, and he lived about a thousand years before Jesus!

The prophetic books of the Old Testament make up a large portion of the Bible. As you learn to identify double fulfillment, general prophecies about the future, specific prophecies about the Messiah and visions of the last days, always look for God's purpose and heart in those passages. Even when God severely reprimanded and judged a person or a nation, his desire was always that they would repent and be restored to relationship with him. The prophetic writings reveal much about God's love for people who will or will not repent of their sins. They show the great lengths to which God goes in calling sinners to come to him, despite what they have done in the past.

Prophecies About the End Times

Although many of the prophecies contained in the prophetic books of the Old Testament have already come to pass, some remain to be fulfilled. Remember the analogy of the house on the hill and the mountain behind it? Well, prophecies about the end times are like the mountain behind the hill.

Most of the prophecies about the end times mention the phrase "day of the Lord" that we have already studied. The prophets seem to constantly move back and forth from God's judgment against the world at the end of time to judgment for the specific sin of the Israelites at a definite time. See how this happens in **Micah 1:2-5**.

Attention! Let all the people of the world listen! Let the earth and everything in it hear. The Sovereign LORD is making accusations against you; the LORD speaks from his holy Temple.

Look! The LORD is coming! He leaves his throne in heaven and tramples the heights of the earth. The mountains melt beneath his feet and flow into the valleys like wax in a fire, like water pouring down a hill. And why is this happening? Because of the rebellion of Israel—yes, the sins of the whole nation. Who is to blame for Israel's rebellion? Samaria, its capital city! Where is the center of idolatry in Judah? In Jerusalem, its capital! (NLT)

This passage begins with the coming of the Lord but ends with the specific sin of idolatry in Israel and Judah. There are countless examples of this in Old Testament prophecy. Read Joel chapter one for another crystal clear example of this back and forth use of prophecy. Joel begins with a prophecy about a local locust plague and by verse fourteen Joel is talking about the day of the Lord. Once you understand this almost continual use of double prophecy, much of the Old Testament will become clearer and easier for you to read.

Chapter 8

New Testament History
Matthew – Acts

Just to ease your mind, I want you to know that I'm not going to give you a whole new set of rules for the historical portion of the New Testament. Everything you've learned about culture, geography and archeology in Old Testament history applies to New Testament history. We will need to tweak things just a little bit, however. Let me explain.

When I go to the nearest Starbucks, I have to make sure I order just the right thing. As you know, they specialize in coffee, which means they offer a wide variety to appeal to individual tastes. They also have a range of different liquid flavors to choose from. My wife likes one pump of almond flavor in her coffee. Notice, I said one pump, not one shot. There is a BIG difference between a "pump" and a "shot." A pump is one "pump" of the almond flavor. A "shot" is three pumps (one serving) of the Almond flavor.

The reason I tell you this is to illustrate a point: **The New Testament historical books require a slightly different approach than Old Testament history. The reason is that the Gospels focus on Jesus, the Son of God.** Since they contain the record of his life, teachings, parables, miracles, suffering and resurrection, we need to add a **few special considerations** to keep in mind when reading and interpreting them.

This chapter supplements what we studied earlier about interpreting the Bible's historical sections. For example, remember the ancient Israeli kings in I and II Kings? Sometimes they did what was right, and sometimes they did what was wrong (as a writer may indicate: "He did evil in the sight of the Lord"), but none were perfect.

Conversely, everything Jesus did was right, true, good, holy, unblemished, faithful, wise, etc. get the picture? There's no evaluation to be made of Jesus — simply submission and acceptance. Of course, Christians read the teachings of Jesus to understand and apply them; I'm not suggesting that we don't study them intently, but that we study Jesus' teaching and life in a slightly different way than we do Old Testament history. With Old Testament history, we evaluate while we read and apply. With Jesus, we bow down on the ground and accept as we read and apply. Sometimes the people in the Old Testament provide an example for us NOT to follow. God allowed the Bible to contain their record so that we wouldn't do some of the things they did. With the teaching of Jesus, however, that is never the case.

To help you gain a proper context for how the Gospel writers wrote their biographies of Jesus, it's important to understand a few of the basics of Gospel interpretation.

Ancient Jewish Expectations and the "Son of Man"

Let's travel back in time to ancient Palestine during the time of Jesus. The Jews are chafing under Roman dominion. They're waiting for their promised Messiah. They expect him to rise to power as a political force, a king who will free them from the control of the Roman Empire.

That all makes for some serious misunderstanding regarding the role and function of the Messiah when Jesus came on the scene. To begin, anyone who studies the Gospels for any length of time comes across the striking fact that almost all the characters in the Gospels misunderstood the ministry of Jesus. Even Jesus' closest friends, the disciples, had no idea of his real purpose before he rose from the grave.

This doesn't mean Jesus wasn't a good teacher. Jesus was the master teacher. He was, however, up against some pretty big expectations and misconceptions about the ministry of the messiah.

The situation was similar to the phenomenon of selective listening that takes place in many marriages. As husbands, we sometimes choose to tune in and out of our wives' conversations, depending on the subject matter. For me, add the fact that I have about 30 percent hearing loss, and that makes for some serious miscommunication between my wife and me at times. Part of the problem is that rather than hearing what our wives are really saying, we husbands hear what we want to hear.

That's how it was between Jesus and the Jewish people. Jesus was the Jewish Messiah. He came to free all people from their sins. Unfortunately, the Jews believed that the Messiah would come as a conquering military leader rather than a humble spiritual leader. They focused on the prophecies that portrayed him as the powerful ruler – which he ultimately will be – instead of as the suffering Savior. Therefore, whenever Jesus displayed supernatural qualities and performed miracles, the Jews got the wrong idea. In fact, in **John 6:14-15**, just after Jesus fed five thousand people, they tried to take him by force and make him their king.

Situations like these made it difficult for Jesus to openly proclaim himself as the Messiah. Whenever Jesus did tell one of his followers that he was the Messiah, he also told them not to say anything about it until after he had risen from the dead. This is known in theological circles as "The Messianic Secret."

So, what did Jesus do to combat this false expectation of the messiah? He referred to himself with a divine title that didn't carry the excess baggage of the term "Messiah." Jesus called himself "the Son of Man," so that he could still be true to his character without identifying himself as the Messiah, which would have been detrimental to his ministry.

Jesus referred to himself more as the Son of Man than anything else. Just look at some of the times he called himself this name in the gospel of Matthew alone. **Matthew 8:20, 12:8, 13:41, 16:13, 17:9, 19:28, 20:18, 24:27, 25:31**. Some take that to mean that Jesus did not believe that he was God. In our day and culture, if someone called himself the Son of Man, we would take that as a reference to his humanness. It's evident in the Scriptures however, that Jesus meant something else entirely by his use of the term.

The first clue that Jesus saw himself as divine appears in **Daniel 7:13-14,** which depicts a divine being that looked like "a son of man," approaching God's throne, being given dominion, power and an everlasting kingdom, and all the peoples of the earth worshiping him. When you read **Mark 14:60-65**, the account Jesus gives of himself to the ruling Jewish leaders is similar to the one in Daniel. This wasn't lost on the Jewish rulers at all. Based on Jesus' words in verse 62, they condemn him to death with the charge of blasphemy (someone claiming to be God).

Jesus' use of the title Son of Man is just one way Jesus' unique relationship with God begins to stand out. Even if he didn't call himself the Messiah a lot, the Gospels paint a clear picture that Jesus believed himself to be the Son of God.

Another interesting example is found in **John 1:51** where Jesus says to his disciples, *"You will see the angels of God ascending and descending on the Son of Man."* Based on the context of Jesus' conversation with Nathanael in the preceding verses, this is a clear reference to Genesis 28. In **Genesis 28:10-17** Jacob has a dream in which he sees the angels of God ascending and descending on a ladder from earth to heaven, with God at the top. And here in John 1, Jesus says that the angels of God will ascend and descend on HIM! If Jesus is not God, he's blaspheming big time! He's putting himself in the place of God, as the one on whom the angels wait.

The Gospels also give other clues about how Jesus perceived himself and his ministry. The following three points will help you as you read about Jesus' teaching and miracles. Remember that the goal here is to learn how to read the gospels productively and worship God as you do.

1. Jesus' teaching must always be taken as authoritative. I know I went over this at the beginning of the chapter, but it bears repeating. When we read about Jesus teaching the crowds or the disciples, we must accept what he says without question.

This is different than some of the people in Old Testament stories. When a king in an Old Testament story speaks, we may understand what he is saying but disagree with him. This is because some historical narrative in the Bible merely records what happened; it doesn't always tell us whether or not to agree with it. With everyone else in Scripture besides Jesus, we can determine from the story and the context whether or not what they did or said was right and whether or not we should imitate them.

With Jesus, however, whatever he says or teaches is true by definition because he is God. When Jesus says, "You shall love your neighbor as yourself," he means it. It's something we are to do, not something we are to weigh in the balance. God's intent is that we submit to it, not find a way to interpret it so that we don't have to deal with it.

Jesus does say some hard things in the gospels. There are times when we are not sure how to apply his teaching, although we believe it. Jesus said *"If your hand causes you to sin, cut it off."* **Matthew 5:30**. Jesus did not intend for us to take this literally, but to literally follow the principle of what he was communicating. In this case, do whatever you have to do to get rid of sin in your life.

2. Jesus' miracles provide insight into God's character. One thing you can always count on is that Jesus' miracles have something to teach us.

I don't mean that we should "over-interpret" every aspect of each miracle, but that usually God has something significant for us to interpret and apply based on Jesus' compassion to heal the sick. For instance, in **John 9:1-34**, when Jesus healed the blind man, he made mud to apply to the man's eyes. I don't know exactly what significance the mud had, but I do know that he performed this miracle on the Sabbath, the day of rest when the Jews were not allowed to work. Spitting was prohibited on the Sabbath because whoever spit would be tempted to cover it up with the dust from his feet – and in the minds of the Jewish leaders, that would be working. So Jesus took the opportunity to arouse the anger of the Pharisees by performing a miracle on the Sabbath in a way that upset them.

Therefore, I learn from this story that God cares more about making people well than about outward, man-made rules. Do you see the point? I can understand the significance of the healing by meditating on the context and details of the passage. In fact, **John 9:13-14** help us tremendously: *"Then they took the man who had been blind to the Pharisees, because it was on the Sabbath that Jesus had made the mud and healed him."* The Pharisees were looking for a way to get Jesus in trouble and when he made mud, they found it. Even though it got him into further trouble with the religious leaders, Jesus specifically chose to heal a man in a way that defied man made religious rules. Since Jesus acted in this way, we begin to see God's heart for healing rather than religious do's and don'ts.

3. Jesus' suffering and resurrection are the primary events in the New Testament. The apostle Paul tells us in I Corinthians 15 that if Jesus did not rise from the dead, our faith is useless and we are still spiritually dead in our sins. Although the Gospel writers report in detail on the events of the weekend of Jesus' death without saying a lot about its spiritual meaning, the rest of the New Testament focuses on the events of that weekend as the most significant in history. The Gospels give us the facts of the story and the rest of the New Testament tells us about the meaning of that weekend.

Therefore, the second half of each Gospel story contains "the heart of the story." This doesn't mean they're "more" inspired than the rest of Scripture, but that all of Scripture finds its purpose in the actual historical story of Jesus' death and resurrection. What does this mean for the student of the Bible? It means that we must see the Old Testament and the New Testament through the lens of this significance. We will not be correctly interpreting and reading Scripture if we miss the fact that the death and resurrection of Jesus is the most important thing.

Background Material for Teaching a Bible Study

When you set out to study a certain book of the Bible, it's good to have background material on the book because it gives you a "head start," if you will, for understanding the book. For that reason, I am providing here two case studies, one for each of the New Testament history sections (the Gospels and Acts).

Looking to the historical and the literary aspects and compiling notes from different sources, I've written the following information that is useful for an in-depth study of two of the New Testament history books, the Gospel of Mark and the book of Acts.

This material is good to have when you begin so that you correctly interpret the text as you read or teach through the book. No matter what Biblical book you are studying, useful background information can be found in commentaries and Bible dictionaries or encyclopedias. Ask your pastor which ones he would recommend you use as you study.

Case Study for New Testament History: Background on the Gospel of Mark[3]

The person who wrote this Gospel was probably John Mark. He is mentioned in **Acts 12:12** and possibly in **Mark 14:51-52**. Some scholars point out that early church history records that Mark wrote down many of Peter's later sermons about Jesus and compiled them into the Gospel of Mark. Therefore, Mark's gospel is really told through the eyes of Peter.

The Gospel of Mark was written sometime after Peter's death, which took place in Rome about 62-63 AD. Not long thereafter, probably between 63 and 66 AD, Mark composed his book.

Mark wrote his Gospel for Roman Christians, who desired that Mark write down Peter's sermons. Mark's emphasis seems to be on Jesus' actions under stress and duress –as God's son yet having to suffer — as the chosen Messiah but having to "keep it a secret" in a sense. The early Roman church would have needed this because they were suffering intense persecution under Nero.

How Jesus handled the persecution he faced without sinning would have been instructive to these Christians. Including the detail that Jesus was in the wilderness *"with the wild animals"* **Mark 1:13**, which no other Gospel mentions, might have been of comfort to Christians who were being fed to the wild animals in the Coliseum at Rome.

We find more clues to Mark's audience when he explains Jewish traditions in **Mark 7:3-5, 14:12, 15:42**. This would have been unnecessary if his audience was Jewish. Mark translates the terms used for money into language a Roman audience would understand, **Mark 12:42**. Mark translates Aramaic and Hebrew expressions into Greek: **Mark 3:17, 5:41, 7:34, 9:43, 10:46, 14:36, 15:22 and 34.** On the other hand, Mark does not explain quotes from the Old Testament prophets, so we can assume that his readers had some understanding of Old Testament literature.

Clues to Peter as a source for Mark's writing include:

Mark 6:45-52 – Mark does *not* mention that Peter walked on the water to meet Jesus. The other Gospel writers do. Peter was humble about this experience, but the other Gospel writers would have wanted to include it in their accounts of the event.

Mark 8: 27-30 – Mark does *not* record Jesus' praise of Peter after Peter's confession of Jesus as the Christ. Again, Peter would have been humble about this, but the other Gospel writers put it in their Gospels.

Mark 16:7 – Mark includes the angel's command to Mary to tell the disciples "and Peter" about the resurrection of Jesus.

These passages support the theory that Peter heavily influenced Mark's writing of this Gospel. Peter, in humility, would not have focused on himself when relating these stories, while the other Gospel writers simply recorded what happened and included Peter's role.

Note also that Mark includes many instances of Jesus rebuking Peter, something not likely to be included if the writer had not been instructed by Peter himself. Other writers would not have highlighted the faults of an early leader of the church like Peter yet leave out his victories of faith. As the testimony from early church history and evidence from the Gospel of Mark come together, it makes sense to see Peter as the source, or voice, for much of Mark's eyewitness material.

Case Study for New Testament History: Background on the Book of Acts

Acts is unique in the Bible because it's the only divinely inspired historical link between the ministry of Jesus and the letters of the New Testament. Acts records how the Church started and spread.

"In my former book Theophilus..." One of the first things we encounter in studying Acts is that both Acts and Luke are addressed to a man named **Theophilus**. It was a common practice during that time period for authors to address their works to a particular person. The book would then be read to that person's intellectual group or community. So although Luke wrote to a person, he knew that his book would be read to a wider audience.

The author of Luke and Acts never explicitly identifies himself, but a number of passages in Acts written in the first person provide clues to the authorship: "**we** went here with Paul" signaling the author is with Paul's group, instead of "they went here and did this." Some such passages are **Acts 16:10-17, 20:5-21:18, 27:1-28:16**. Whoever wrote the book traveled with Paul, and we know from Paul's letters that Luke was with him on many occasions. Paul even mentions Luke as a friend and co-worker in **Col. 4:14, II Timothy 4:11 and Philemon 24**.

Ancient church history identifies Luke the doctor as the author. **Eusebius**, the great church historian in the 300s AD, wrote that Luke was a physician from Antioch, a place where Paul served after being converted. Eusebius says that Luke was the author.

A second century church father, **Irenaeus**, wrote that Paul and Luke were inseparable. So although his name is not given in either book, enough clues in the text and explicit references in church history indicate clearly that Luke wrote Acts.

In addition to traveling extensively with Paul, Luke interviewed many people in writing his gospel and he knew the other apostles well. He was an educated Christian man who investigated the claims made by the people who knew Jesus and wrote down his conclusions, **Luke 1:1-3**.

Acts and Luke are the two longest books in the New Testament. Each fits well on a scroll about 35 feet long, which was about the largest you could obtain in the first century. It's also interesting that during that time period it was considered a stylistic achievement to make each volume of a multi-volume work about equal length.

It's clear from the writing style and quality that an educated person wrote Acts. Luke was a doctor, and he paid special attention to medical details in his writing. He also revealed his seafaring experience in his use of Greek nautical terms in Acts 27 and 28. In all, we find a refined, educated, scholarly Christian man writing a book to persuade others of the truths of God that he has become convinced of.

Since Luke wrote Acts as historical narrative, his book can rightfully be called history. Yet it is history with a special point, a theological point, a point about a spiritual reality, so it is not just history for history's sake. He definitely has a perspective just as everyone who records history has a perspective.

Many liberal scholars in the late eighteenth and early nineteenth centuries originally thought that Luke wrote long after the events in question happened, even as late as 150 AD or so, a hundred years after some of the events in Acts. Yet scholars have now confirmed that Luke actually lived in the first century AD, when the events recorded in Acts happened.

One of the great historians who made this discovery was **Sir William Ramsey (1851-1939)**. Ramsey was a lecturer in Archeology and Classical Art at Oxford University when he set out to the Middle East for archaeological work. At this time, archeology was just in its beginning stages as a field of history. Since no maps of the New Testament era existed, he made his own by studying ancient historical sources.

When he began his journey, he believed, as many of his day did, that Luke and the rest of the New Testament were not accurate. The longer his journey went on, however, the more he came to rely on the historical details that Luke provided as opposed to other ancient sources. He eventually wrote:

*The more I have studied the narrative of Acts and the more
I have learned year after year about Greco-Roman society
thoughts and fashions, and organization in those provinces,*

*the more I admire and the better I understand. I set out to
look for truth in the borderland where Greece and Asia meet,
and found it here [in Acts]. <u>You may press the words of Luke
in a degree beyond any other historian's and they stand the
keenest scrutiny and the hardest treatment.</u>"* **4**

If you desire to read Sir William Ramsey's work, his best book
on the subject is ***St. Paul: Traveler and Roman Citizen.***

Understanding Jesus' life and teaching in addition to the unique
background of each gospel and Acts will help you as you grow in
your ability to learn and apply the Word of God. In this next chapter,
we will consider a form of teaching given by Jesus called parables.
They make up a significant portion of the gospels. Understanding
the parables will lift your Biblical interpretation skills to the next
level.

Chapter 9

Jesus' Parables
Found in the Gospels of Matthew,
Mark, Luke and John

Who was Jesus? He was a storyteller... he was the world's greatest storyteller. Ask him a question; he'd answer with a story. Give him a crowd of people listening intently; he told them stories. Give him an argument; he'd give you a story. Give him a real tricky, catchy question; he'd give you a real tricky, catchy story. Have you ever watched a seven-year-old listening — inhaling — a story? Eyes wide, mouth slung open, mind churning... he is totally absorbed. This man-God Jesus...he knew what he was doing. **5**

Jesus told simple stories that illustrated great spiritual truths. He told stories that everybody could relate to.

Jesus' stories are still with us today. Read the parable of the Prodigal Son in **Luke 15:11-32** or the story of the Good Samaritan in **Luke 10:29-37**. Jesus taught in an unforgettable way. Imagine making up a simple story that will be remembered two thousand years from now. In the year 4008 A.D., people still read and understand your story. That is absolutely crazy! And yet Jesus did it more than once!

Jesus of Nazareth was the greatest teacher who ever lived. His crystal clear style communicated exactly what he wanted you to know. In fact, the rest of us who call ourselves Christian preachers and teachers still rock in his wake and struggle just to get out the right words so that we don't mess up what he was saying to the people around him.

As you think about Jesus' parables, it is important to remember that they are not complicated. Most of the parables that Jesus told were designed to illustrate a point in his teaching or give an example of a spiritual truth.

For this reason, you shouldn't read too much into a parable's details. The meaning of most parables becomes apparent when you note the context in which Jesus gave them. A good example is the parable of the wicked tenants in **Matthew 21:33-46**. Matthew tells us that even Jesus' enemies understood that he directed this parable against them and their behavior. So don't overanalyze the parables. Receive them, take them in and absorb them. *Allow them to form word pictures in your mind.*

Always remember to read the immediate context surrounding these incredible stories. Many times, the immediate context gives you the point of the parable. The Gospel writers help us do this. For instance, in **Luke 10:25-37**, we find Jesus teaching on the need to love your neighbor. A man asks him, *"Teacher, who then is my neighbor?"* Jesus responds with the parable of the Good Samaritan.

In Jesus' time, Jews hated Samaritans, and the feeling was mutual. So Jesus tells a story about a Jew who gets mugged and left for dead. Two Jewish religious men pass by him without stopping to help. Then a Samaritan man comes by, stops to help, bandages his wounds and pays for his recovery at the local hotel. Jesus even strengthens this example by saying, *"Then a __despised__ Samaritan came along, and when he saw the man, he felt compassion for him"* (Luke 10:33, emphasis mine). Jesus' radical answer to the question, "who is my neighbor?" makes it clear that even someone we consider an enemy is our neighbor. Way to go, Jesus!

The Two Purposes of Jesus' Parables:
1. To give simple, easily understood examples of his spiritual lessons.
2. To separate those who wanted to follow him from those who didn't.

Although Jesus designed many of his parables to amplify his sermons, sometimes he used parables for another purpose: to weed out people who weren't really interested in his ministry. One key parable that serves this purpose is found in **Matthew 13:1-23**. I've decided to go through this parable verse by verse so that you can get a good idea of how to interpret the parable itself. This will also give you a heads-up on how to interpret the other parables that Jesus used to discern his true followers.

Matthew 13:1-23

(Vs. 1) That same day Jesus went out of the house and sat by the lake.

Since you've learned that the context of any biblical passage is important, here's some quick background compiled from Matthew and the other gospels about this day. This is the same day that Jesus' mother and brothers had tried to get in to see him because they thought things were getting out of control in Jesus' ministry. It's also the same day that he had debated with the Scribes and the Pharisees about who he was and why he came in the first place. The Pharisees wanted to see a sign, but Jesus wouldn't give them one.

It must be getting late in the afternoon, and Jesus just keeps going. In fact, he is about to give some of his most remembered teaching — the parables about the Kingdom of Heaven. Matthew 13 contains seven parables that illustrate various aspects of the Kingdom of Heaven.

The kingdom of God or the "kingdom of Heaven" as Matthew calls it, refers to God's reign over this earth. **Revelation 21:3** tells us that God will come one day and set up his kingdom to make his dwelling place with us forever. His reign on earth has already begun through us who believe that Jesus is the Messiah. We are his divine agents of salvation, sent out to gather anyone who also wants to join God's kingdom.

(Vs. 2) Such large crowds gathered around him that he got into a boat and sat in it, while all the people stood on the shore.

The house Jesus taught from earlier in the day was so crowded that his mom and brothers couldn't even get inside. When he goes outside, the crowd grows larger and presses around him there, too. He decides to get into a boat in order to give himself some space. This provided a good place to teach and a nice acoustic setting for a lot of people to hear his message.

This phase of Jesus' ministry is often called the "popular phase." During this time in his ministry, Jesus often spoke to crowds of more than a thousand people at one time. In addition to being physically strong (remember, he was a carpenter), Jesus must have had a powerful speaking voice as well, since the ancient world didn't have microphones.

(Vs. 3) Then he told them many things in parables, saying: "A farmer went out to sow his seed."

Jesus used word pictures that people in his day immediately understood. Not all of them were farmers, but all of them lived in an agricultural society. They all knew farming and saw it taking place near their homes. Jesus relates to the people's situation. He doesn't approach them with high-minded theological truth, but with lowly, thoughtful stories that instantly created pictures in their minds.

(Vs. 4) "As he was scattering the seed, some fell along the path, and the birds came and ate it up."

This is how sowing seed was done in Jesus' day. The farmer walked through a field with a sack of grain over his shoulder. He threw out handfuls of grain and allowed the wind to spread the seeds. He plowed the ground only after he had sown the seed.

(Vss. 5-9) "Some fell on rocky places, where it did not have much soil. It sprang up quickly because the soil was shallow. But when the sun came up, the plants were scorched, and they withered because they had no root. Other seed fell among thorns, which grew up and choked the plants. Still other seed fell on good soil, where it produced a crop — a hundred, sixty or thirty times what was sown. He who has ears to hear, let him hear."

Some of us were raised going to church or have been Christians for a while, and we have a tendency to go right to the application and interpretation of Jesus' stories. I encourage you to stop for a moment and think about what Jesus really did by telling this story and then moving right on to the next story without giving his audience any explanation.

It was like this: Imagine your pastor stood up on Sunday morning and said,

"I knew a man who bought a new car the other day. As he drove it away from the dealership it started to rain. The rain began to get on his shirt, so naturally he rolled up the windows. But even after he rolled up the windows, the rain trickled into the car and onto his sleeve. In the end, his entire shirt got soaked. Please think about what I have said today. And now we'll have the closing prayer."

You'd think, "What's going on here?" Naturally you would wonder about the meaning of the story. Some people in the service would leave and go to lunch with others in the church and agree that the preacher was off his rocker, while others would stick around to find out the meaning of the story.

It was the same with people when Jesus lived on earth. The ministry of Jesus was enormously popular and large numbers of people followed him, but they didn't all follow him for the same reasons. Some people followed him just because he fed them. In fact, the Gospel of John mentions that Jesus told the people, *"You are not following me to see a sign but because you ate and were filled"* **John 6:26**.

Jesus didn't want people following him just for self-serving reasons, so he told parables to find out who was curious and would ask for more information. Did they follow him because they were expecting the Messiah of Israel, or did they just want to have their physical needs met or see a "circus side-show" of miracles?

> **(Vss. 10-12) The disciples came to him and asked, "Why do you speak to the people in parables?" He replied, "The knowledge of the secrets of the kingdom of heaven has been given to you, but not to them. Whoever has will be given more, and he will have abundance. Whoever does not have, even what he has will be taken from him."**

Jesus alternated between public teaching and private instruction as **Mark 4:33** shows: *"With many such parables he was speaking the word to them as much as they were able to bear it, and he did not speak to them without a parable, but he was explaining everything privately to his own disciples."* This is an important point to recognize. If you don't see this, then later on Jesus might look like he doesn't care for the people. Recognize that parables, among other things, were a teaching device to separate those who were really interested from those who didn't care too much. So we see in Matthew 13 that Jesus is explaining this parable about sowing seed to more than just the twelve disciples. Anybody who really wanted to follow Jesus got the inside scoop.

His disciples were the ones who came to him afterward seeking to understand, seeking to know more and he readily revealed himself to them. The more someone sought the truth, the more truth was given to them. Jesus was honest about the fact that the disciples got more information than everybody else. Verses 10-12 refer not just to the twelve disciples, but a group that numbered around a hundred or so. To illustrate how many close followers Jesus had, at one point in his ministry Jesus sent out seventy-two followers at once to announce the good news **Luke 10:1**.

And here it is, don't miss this! Jesus says in verse 12, "Whoever has will be given more and whoever does not have, even what he thinks he has will be taken from him." Those who want to find out more about the kingdom get more of the kingdom. Those who do not want much to do with it will not get any of it.

> **(Vss. 13-15) "That is why I speak to them in parables; though seeing, they do not see; though hearing they do not hear or understand. In them is fulfilled the prophecy of Isaiah: "'You will be ever hearing but never understanding; you will be ever seeing but never perceiving. For this people's heart has become calloused; they hardly hear with their ears and they have closed their eyes. Otherwise they might see with their eyes, hear with their ears, understand with their hearts and turn and I would heal them.'"**

The Bible teaches that someone can reach a point where they no longer understand or appreciate the truth because they have knowingly blinded themselves to it for so long. Eventually God gives a person like that over to their own evil desires. Jesus says that these people actually see him teach and hear his words but they don't recognize who he is and they don't understand his words because they don't truly want to know him. **Verse 15** puts it clearly: *"For this people's heart has become calloused."* The New Testament cites this passage at least six times in describing people who did not want to understand the message of salvation. We can choose to shut our ears to it. We can allow it to pass over our heads. We can shut our eyes to it if we really want to.

> **(Vs. 16) "But blessed are your eyes because they see, and your ears because they hear."**

Just as some do not hear, other people do. In **John 14:21** Jesus says, *"He who loves me will be loved by my Father, and I will love him and will reveal myself to him."*

Jesus pronounced a blessing upon these disciples. For all their flaws, they had some sense of how significant Jesus was. Here's a point to consider. You don't need to know everything about Jesus in order to come to him. These disciples still had some misconceptions about Jesus, but that didn't stop Jesus from blessing them. It didn't stop them from following him because they recognized that he was different from everyone else who had ever lived.

(Vs. 17) "For I tell you the truth, many prophets and righteous men longed to see what you see but did not see it, and to hear what you hear but did not hear it."

Jesus now informs them that many righteous people who came before them greatly desired to see the Messiah but did not get to. As the Old Testament character Job said, *"Oh that I could have a mediator stand between myself and God."* There before the disciples was the fulfillment of Job's cry, standing on earth in human flesh: Jesus the Son of God.

Isaiah wrote, *"And you shall call his name Immanuel, which means God with us."* As God told Abraham, *"All the nations of the earth shall be blessed through you."* There with the disciples stood that blessing. Many God-fearing, faithful people looked forward to the time of the Messiah, and did not live to see it, but this group of rag-tag followers did. Jesus is the fulfillment of all the Old Testament promises.

(Vs. 18) "Listen then to what the parable of the sower means."

Not only did Jesus tell the disciples more about himself but he also explained the parable for them. They didn't really ask for the interpretation, they asked why he spoke to the people in parables. For all their flaws, the disciples stayed with Jesus when the crowds went away. They weren't satisfied with distant crowd contact with

Jesus; they wanted deeper, more intimate fellowship with him, and he gave it to them. He did not turn away any who desired it. He explained the parable to those who really wanted to stay with him.

(Vs. 19) "When anyone hears the message about the kingdom and does not understand it, the evil one comes and snatches away what was sown in his heart. This is the seed sown along the path."

The good news goes out to all people. The other Gospels tell us that in this parable the one who sows seed is actually sowing the Word of God.

In this verse Jesus didn't mean someone who cannot intellectually understand the message such as someone who may be mentally disabled. He meant someone to whom the gospel just doesn't make sense. **I Corinthians 1:23** says that the gospel was just plain foolishness to the Greeks. That meant that they just couldn't accept that God would come down in human form and die for people. Their concept of God was too far removed from that idea. They couldn't reconcile it with what they thought they already knew about God.

If someone doesn't understand or accept the gospel, the enemy steals the seed away from his heart. This occurs because the person's heart is not right before God. The person holds on to his pride and won't allow God to "interfere" with his life.

(Vss. 20-21) "The one who received the seed that fell on rocky places is the man who hears the word and at once receives it with joy. But since he has no root, he lasts only a short time. When trouble or persecution comes because of the word, he quickly falls away."

You may know of people who go forward at an evangelistic crusade or say "yes" to Jesus but then later on seem to drift away or outright renounce their once joyful faith. In this passage, the Greek uses the term **euthus** (immediately) to describe both the quickness in coming to the faith and quickness in leaving the faith. Easy come, easy go.

Since immediate gratification usually wins out, they want nothing to do with the hard things that come along with the gospel.

How did these "plants" wither away? They got scorched by the hot sun (verse 6) and withered. Jesus interprets the sun coming up as trouble or persecution; notice in the parable that these "plants" have no root. They are not really anchored to Christ. They made a change because they thought it was what was good for them at the time but they didn't have the anchor that holds in stormy times. They made a decision based on their feelings rather than faith, and feelings change all the time. They didn't have the rock of faith as the solid foundation to hold them in trouble. They didn't have the root of salvation, Jesus Christ. They could not overcome their emotions, both in coming to Jesus, and then in leaving him later when life got tough. They had no real "roots" in Christ.

(Vs. 22) "The one who received the seed that fell among the thorns is the man who hears the word, but the worries of this life and the deceitfulness of wealth choke it, making it unfruitful."

Just as the group in verses 20-21 withered from outside conditions (the hot son), this group is made unfruitful by its own ground. Think of the soil as the disposition of the heart. It is what we are deep inside ourselves that no one ever knows about but us. It is who we are when no one else sees us.

These people receive the gospel, but eventually other things in their hearts that they have not dealt with consume them and keep them from growing in Christ. Sometimes worry or fear overcomes faith in God. It may be the fear of death, the fear of losing a loved one, or the fear of not being able to support your family. Any fear that resides in the same heart where the gospel resides must be dealt with. If not, the enemy will eventually find a way to exploit it and use it against the believer. When some people lose a loved one, they cast off their belief in God because the thing they feared most has come to pass. **II Timothy 1:7** tells us that *"God did not give us a spirit of fear but of power and love and a sound mind."* All Christians go through some tremendously painful things in this life, but God does not want fear and worry to control us. The writer of Hebrews encourages us to *"throw off the sin that so easily entangles and run with perseverance the race set before us."* **Hebrews 12:1**

Additionally, Jesus tells us that the deceitfulness of wealth can also make someone unfruitful. Notice he does not say wealth itself does this. The deceitfulness of wealth is the belief that wealth will solve your problems and give you worth. Such beliefs drive a person on a vicious search for more wealth, more power, and more control, instead of turning to God in true submission. Tribulation, persecution, worry, the deceitfulness of riches, these are things that can turn people from God.

(Vs. 23) "But the one who received the seed that fell on good soil is the man who hears the word and understands it. He produces a crop, yielding a hundred, sixty or thirty times what was sown."

This portrays the person who hears the gospel, understands it, and lives it. This person produces fruit. This person's fruit may be a hundred times greater than what the one seed would have produced. This is the case with many who come to know Christ. They lead lives that are so fruitful they are like well-watered trees that bring forth fruit at all times.

We have a tendency to recoil from this parable because it so clearly relays that the only people who are saved are the ones who produce fruit. But this is totally in accordance with the Christian message. **James 2:14-26** tells us that our faith should be seen by the good things that we do. We are not saved *by* works but *for* good works. Everyone who is saved will eventually produce fruit, showing Jesus' parable to be true. The control of Jesus will be evident in their lives.

This parable points to the tension we feel when we read many of Jesus' parables. They make us think, they leave us with a certainty that sometimes scares us in its blunt truth, yet they leave room for an alternate ending for those who change their ways.

Jesus' teaching is at its most direct in his parables. They are simple stories with real-life application. These stories about simple agricultural life in Palestine two thousand years ago still hit us full force — proving the reality of our Savior's unmatched teaching ability.

Chapter 10

New Testament Epistles
Romans – Jude

W hen my oldest daughter was seven years old, she wrote a letter to the president of the United States. A few months later, she got a response from the White House. While it was not from the president himself, it was from someone in his office and included a picture of the president.

My daughter was awestruck at having received a response from the White House. As an adult, I was thinking, "The White House staff _has_ to do this type of stuff." But my daughter was on a different plane of reality. She probably told everyone she knew that she got a letter from the White House.

That got me thinking. What if we really got a response directly from the president himself? We would cherish it. As Christians, we have something better: letters to us from the apostles themselves, guided directly by the Holy Spirit.

It may be helpful for you to think of an epistle as an "apostle letter," letters from the apostles or brothers of Jesus to a church or churches. Even in the early Church, false teaching abounded, so it was important that the apostles stay in contact with the churches they started.

Many times, Paul felt compelled to write to a certain church because they were being led astray by some false teaching. In Thessalonica, someone was teaching that the Second Coming of

Jesus had already happened and the believers had missed it. In Galatia, someone had begun teaching that the Christians had to obey the Law of Moses in order to be saved. Many of the epistles responded to problems that specific churches were experiencing.

Did You Know?

**The apostles wrote two kinds of epistles or letters:
First, they sent letters to churches.
The apostle addressed entire congregations and meant for
the letter to be read out loud. Most of the letters
in the New Testament are this kind.
Second, they wrote personal letters to someone they knew.
Paul wrote four of these: I and II Timothy, Titus and
Philemon. John wrote two: II and III John.**

Apostles wrote two kinds of epistles: letters to churches and letters to individuals. Letters to individuals (i.e., I and II Timothy) are by nature more personal and conversational. Letters to churches (i.e., Philippians) are more formal. This is not an ironclad principle, just a general distinction.

In terms of ancient letter writing, all the biblical epistles fall more on the conversational or informal side. To help you get a grip on the flow of a biblical letter, I've written the general outline most of the letters use. Because Paul wrote more epistles than anybody else, we'll use his writing as a model. You will see this general pattern in most of the other epistles. An epistle usually includes the following elements:

1. An opening greeting.

The author of an epistle tells who he is and why he has the authority to write to the church. When Paul writes, *"Paul, called to be an apostle..."* he isn't doing it to remind himself of his credentials; he's doing it to remind the church of his credentials. It was important that the church respect Paul's authority as a leader and put into practice the teaching contained in the letter.

Also in the opening greeting, the author makes clear who the letter is addressed to. In the early church, the apostles wrote letters to many churches. These letters were so important that the recipients sent copies to other churches as well. Paul even wrote in **Colossians 4:16**, *"After this letter has been read to you, see that it is also read in the church of the Laodiceans and that you in turn read the letter from Laodicea."* So it was important to remember which church the letter addressed in the first place.

The greeting set the tone of the letter. It reminded the church that the person writing to them had been called to be an apostle by the Lord Jesus himself.

In most of the epistles the writer follows his introduction with a brief greeting to the church. Paul used the phrase *"grace and peace to you."* Paul wanted to establish that he loved the people in the church. God the Father bestowed grace on us through Jesus and we have obtained peace from God as a result of coming to him through Jesus. Additionally, some commentators suggest that the Greeks used the word "grace" to greet one another and the Jews used "peace" when greeting one another, so Paul combined them both into a Christian greeting.

2. A Thanksgiving or Blessing.

Most epistles open with a prayer or a blessing from the apostle, not to the church, but to God. **I Peter 1:3-5** states:

Blessed be the God and Father of our Lord Jesus Christ! According to his great mercy, he has caused us to be born again to a living hope through the resurrection of Jesus Christ from the dead, to an inheritance that is imperishable, undefiled, and unfading, kept in heaven for you, who by God's power are being guarded through faith for a salvation ready to be revealed in the last time.

In blessing God, Peter shows the church how wonderful their salvation is. He praises God for the things God has done for the church. These words of blessing, or thanksgiving, teach Christians a great deal about theology, the character of God and salvation.

Read the verse above again and think about what Peter is saying. From this verse alone you can be sure about your inheritance in heaven. You can know that you are being guarded through faith for the eternal life that God is bringing with him when he reveals himself to the world at the Second Coming. Peter also tells you that being born again is being born to a living hope. All of the hope that you have is bound up in the resurrection of Christ.

When you read the epistles, don't skip the blessings. They're a rich source for learning all God has done for us.

Paul records a shorter thanksgiving in **Romans 1:8**: *"First, I thank my God through Jesus Christ for all of you, because your faith is proclaimed in all the world."* Paul was commending the church. Rome was a large city, and word of the church in Rome spread to all the known parts of the Mediterranean world. Paul was extremely thankful for this. He was thankful to see such a strong church in a large city. It was a sign to him that Christianity was spreading all over the world. Additionally, people throughout the Mediterranean world who traveled to Rome had a chance to encounter Christians and get saved.

As you study the epistles, you will notice subtle differences in the letters. For instance, in Galatians, Paul gives no thanksgiving prayer or blessing. He gets right to his point. His message was so urgent that he skipped a section that is in all his other letters. He was deeply upset that the church in Galatia was listening to false teachers. These false teachers were leading the church back into practices of the Old Testament law. Paul hotly refutes the idea that anyone must obey the law to be saved. This opens a window on the first-century world. It shows some of the false teaching of that day. It also shows what matters to the heart of God.

Since the Holy Spirit is the ultimate author of the book, you see Paul's heart and God's heart toward those who would be saved by faith and then try to be made right by following the law. *"Let me ask you only this: Did you receive the Spirit by works of the law or by hearing with faith? Are you so foolish? Having begun by the Spirit, are you now being perfected by the flesh?"* **Galatians 3:2-3**

Paul used several arguments in the short letter of Galatians to prove his point, and all of them get right at the law vs. grace dispute. The tone of the entire book is set from the beginning, and starts with the lack of a thanksgiving or blessing from Paul. The book of Galatians is serious throughout. By noticing these details, you get a clearer picture of God's attitude toward the issues that Paul dealt with in the epistle.

3. The Body of the letter. Specific instructions based on what is happening in their church.

Many of the epistles contain teachings from the apostles based on questions or problems that the churches had at the time. They were written for a certain occasion or reason. As I mentioned before, the purpose of the book of Galatians was to refute the teaching of those who wanted the church to go back to following the regulations of the Old Testament Law.

In I Corinthians, Paul answered many questions. It seems that some people in the church at Corinth had come to Paul and told him about the problems in the church. *"For it has been reported to me by Chloe's people that there is quarreling among you, my brothers"* **I Corinthians 1:11**.

As Paul wrote to the church at Corinth, he had to address their problems. The church in Corinth had a LOT of problems. They struggled with immorality, factions, favoritism, gifts of the Spirit, people speaking out of order during meetings of the church, etc. Paul dealt with those problems.

It is always helpful to find out what questions the apostle is answering. You find out what questions Paul is answering by identifying the issues he addressed. If you do this, you will have a much better understanding of the book itself and the ancient Church.

The fact that you have answers to ancient questions instead of modern ones shouldn't cause you to disregard the advice. Even though you might not always ask the same questions, there are times when you do. For instance, many churches still struggle with the proper use of spiritual gifts in public meetings of the church. These questions have been answered in I Corinthians. All Christians still wonder about the timing of the Lord's return. This has been addressed in I and II Thessalonians. Christians still wonder what kind of person ought to hold the office of elder. This question is answered in I Timothy and Titus.

The answers given by the apostles are especially relevant to today's situations. Divorce is prevalent in today's churches. The apostles speak to this in some of the epistles. In fact, the Pastoral Epistles, those books written to individual church leaders, are incredibly relevant for today's pastor. The books of I and II Timothy and Titus hold a treasure chest of wisdom for young pastors in ministry.

The epistles aren't going to answer all your specific questions. They weren't given for that reason. They addressed the questions and problems of specific churches. Once you realize this, however, the closer you come to drawing good conclusions and principles from the issues they dealt with. That brings you closer to solving your own problems. Learning the ancient Church's problems and the principles rightly derived from them helps you begin to understand the scriptural answers to your problems or your church's situations.

When you read Paul's letters, notice his use of rhetorical questions. Many times he asked a question that the reader already knew the answer to. In **I Corinthians 1:13-14**, he asked, *"Is Christ divided? Was Paul crucified for you? Or were you baptized in the name of Paul? I thank God that I baptized none of you except Crispus and Gaius."*

He asked this question to make the Corinthian people realize how foolish it was for them to argue about whether they liked Peter or Paul better. Paul was clear. He said that the only person who matters is Jesus. His rhetorical question, *"Was Paul crucified for you?"* was not meant to be seriously answered but to shock the reader into remembering that only Jesus was crucified for the Church.

Additionally, the apostles used a range of evidence and methods to answer the questions asked of them. Think of it like this: When your teenage daughter comes to you and wants to get a tattoo, you're going to use every piece of available evidence to try to convince her not to get one. You're not going to confine yourself to just one line of argumentation.

You're going to tell her that needles can spread disease and that her arms will get flabby when she gets older and the tattoo will look "different" then. You're going to cite any law from the Old Testament you can find whether or not it really applies. You're going to talk to her about pain tolerance while finding a story on the Internet about some poor schmuck who died while getting a tattoo. OK, this may be a bit of an exaggeration, but this is similar to methods the apostles used. Some of the apostles used a range of arguments to prove their points. They didn't always use the same kinds of arguments, but in the case of the epistles, all their arguments are legitimate.

At times they appealed to the Old Testament. In the book of Hebrews, the author quoted many verses from the Old Testament to show how Jesus perfectly fulfilled all the requirements of the Law, enabling him to become our perfect High Priest.

Some epistles refer to the teachings of Jesus in their advice to the churches. In I Corinthians 11, Paul instructed the Corinthian church on the proper way to observe communion and quoted the words of Jesus. The apostles used examples from nature and creation. Paul did this in I Corinthians 15 regarding the resurrection of the body. In his epistle, James used vivid pictures, from ships to horses to fire, to show the church how dangerous the tongue is.

There were a variety of ways the authors of the epistles got a point across. The authors of the epistles used various methods depending on the point they were trying to prove to the churches.

The epistles, or letters, address a range of questions. They answer questions on such subjects as marriage, communion, speaking in tongues, favoritism, gossip, the qualifications for elders, resolving disagreements among church members, what will happen when Jesus comes back, the difference between works and grace, how to recognize false prophets, how to take care of widows, how to rejoice in suffering, what the Old Testament Tabernacle signified, how to pray for wisdom, submitting to authority, how much Jesus loves us, and how to overcome the world, among other things. Whew! They contain a wealth of incredible information from God himself. Each time I read through them, I'm amazed at what I missed the time before. They get better with each reading!

4. Closing remarks and personal greetings.

Since these are letters to specific people or church groups, the apostle usually closes his letter with final words of wisdom and personal greetings to certain people in the church. At times, we get a glimpse of the concerns or affection the apostle had for the recipient.

In **I Timothy 6:20** Paul ends the letter with an emotional call to his disciple, Timothy: *"Oh Timothy, guard the deposit entrusted to you. Avoid the irreverent babble and contradictions of what is falsely called knowledge."* You can almost hear Paul's voice imploring the young pastor Timothy not to get wrapped up in vain discussions of mythology and Jewish genealogies. Timothy was close to Paul's heart and he wanted Timothy to stay far away from anything having to do with the *"irreverent babble"* coming from some of the false teachers of the day.

The apostles' closing greetings to certain people provide us with crucial information. Paul, especially, took time to mention many people at the end of some of his letters. This reveals whom he sent to minister to the church, who the church leaders were at the time, and what Paul's relationship was with them. The book of Acts, which is history, gives us some details about Paul's travels and ministry, but the letters fill in details that Acts does not give us about Paul's ministry.

Additionally, even if Paul used an Amanuensis (secretary) to write the letter, to prove that the letter was authentic, he would write the last portion himself. For instance, in **Colossians 4: 18** he wrote, *"I, Paul write this greeting with my own hand. Remember my chains. Grace be with you."* Paul was telling them that his signature was on the letter. It was authentic.

The closing remarks of the epistles also gave instructions or requests from the apostle for help, prayer, materials, and volunteers. The book of Romans has one of the longest closing remarks sections;

one half of chapter 15 and all of chapter 16 list Paul's needs and his greetings to the church at Rome.

Now that you have a general idea of the format of ancient letters, here are some principles that will help you understand the message of each letter and how it applies to your life today.

Important Considerations When Reading the Letters

As you learn to interpret Scripture, you will find some general rules and guidelines that give you a general feel for the text most of the time even though they might not hold true *all* of the time.

It's like when my kids ask me if there is any weeding they can do in the backyard. They might want to do it out of the goodness of their hearts, but I usually have a pretty good idea that they're asking because they want money or something else from me. It's the same with interpreting the biblical letters; there might be exceptions, but the following principles apply **most** of the time.

Principle 1: Each letter has one correct interpretation of the writer's message to his original audience.

In **Philippians 4:2-3** Paul wrote,
"I plead with Euodia and I plead with Syntyche to agree with each other in the Lord. Yes, and I ask you, loyal yoke-fellow, help these women who have contended at my side in the cause of the gospel, along with Clement and the rest of my fellow workers, whose names are in the book of life."

It's a pretty easy assumption that the correct interpretation of this passage is that Paul wants the whole church to help these two women to get along. It's clear they had some sort of conflict.

Another example is Paul's admonition for women not to wear jewelry or have braided hair: *"I also want women to dress modestly, with decency and propriety, not with braided hair or gold or pearls or expensive clothes, but with good deeds, appropriate for women who profess to worship God"* **I Timothy 2:8-10**.

117

It helps to know that during that time period, prostitutes sometimes wore braided hair and lots of jewelry. When you understand this, what Paul wrote makes sense. He didn't care about the way a woman wore her hair unless it relayed something that didn't reflect well on a Christian woman. In applying this principle to our modern churches, we still say, "Women should dress modestly." We don't include the part about braided hair because that was directed to Paul's original audience. If there was something in our culture that was a sure "sign" of a prostitute, we would be right in telling women of the church never to wear that sign.

So always remember, there is one correct interpretation of what the author wrote but many correct applications. The original audience doesn't change; it was a church or person in the first century living in a particular time and place. The reason that the application can change is that we live in different life situations, with different cultures and customs than the original church the letter addressed. We're always looking to find the principle from the interpretation that we can then apply to our lives. The pattern can be seen like this:

Original Interpretation → Principle → Modern Application

So, as we study the epistles, how do we know the difference between the cultural traditions that can be applied differently and the overarching principles that do not change? That is where the major disagreements arise. When Paul said *"The women must keep silent in the church"* **I Corinthians 14:34**, we all agree that he meant that for the churches back then, but Christians disagree about whether or not to transfer the principle from that cultural situation into our churches today. In order to help you come to solid conclusions, I will continue with the general principles that will help you as you study the issues yourself.

Principle 2: When an epistle describes an action, an emotional quality or a state of mind that Christians are to strive for, you can assume that it is for you today.

You may have to change the details a bit, such as, "I can find joy in the Lord even though my car broke down," in place of, "I can find joy even though I'm stuck in a Roman prison." That's my modern translation of **Philippians 1:12-14**! All kidding aside, the principle always carries over.

As people, we've been created with certain natural responses to good and bad situations, and the responses are the same no matter what age we live in. When we are persecuted, we are tempted to give up. When we are insulted, we are tempted to strike back. When we are slandered, we are tempted to slander back.

It doesn't matter that Paul wrote the command *"Do not lie to one another"* **Colossians 3:9,** two thousand years ago — I comprehend right away what Paul meant. Some things don't change. Or, when I read in **Romans 12: 1-2**, *"Do not be conformed to this world, but be transformed by the renewal of your mind, that by testing you may discern what is the will of God, what is good and acceptable and perfect,"* without much work, I realize that God desires my mind to be separate from the sinful things that go on here in the world. He wants me to be transformed to be more like Christ and less like the world around me.

These are just a couple examples of how the epistles are immediately helpful to your Christian walk without having to do a lot of in-depth research about culture or history. So that you really get the point, consider **Galatians 5:22-23**, *"the fruit of the Spirit is love, joy, peace, patience, kindness, goodness, faithfulness, gentleness and self-control. There is no law against such things."* In God's kingdom, you cannot go wrong with these qualities, no matter when or where you live.

So remember, when the an author directs his readers to have an emotional quality in a certain situation, as in **James 1:2-3**, *"Count it all joy, my brothers, when you meet trials of various kinds, for you know that the testing of your faith produces steadfastness,"* you know it applies to us today just as it did two thousand years ago. We need to act on the command. No matter what kind of trial we face, we are to count it all joy, because when our faith is tested, it produces a steadfast character.

Principle 3: When the writer of an epistle appeals to the character of God when giving a command or direction to his readers, that command is timeless and applies to us today.

For instance, Paul was encouraging Christians to be completely humble and gentle when he wrote in **Philippians 2: 5-7a**, *"Your attitude should be the same that Christ Jesus had. Though he was God, he did not demand and cling to his rights as God. He made himself nothing…"*

Paul appealed to his readers to be humble by citing the character of Jesus when he lived on earth. Jesus laid aside his glory and humbly served us by ministering to us and then dying for us. Such a command transcends culture and time.

When an apostle appeals to the character of God, there is no room for us to say, "Well, he meant that back then, but not for today." There is no situation that allows for us not to be humble and gentle because the attitude of Christ during his entire time on earth was one of humility.

Another example where a writer cites the character of God in order to correct Christian thinking is **James 1:13**: *"Let no one say when he is tempted, 'I am being tempted by God,' for God cannot be tempted with evil, and he himself tempts no one."* James tells us, "You can't say that God brought this temptation your way, because God doesn't do that sort of thing." No matter what age we live in, we can never say "God wanted me to sin" because the character of God never changes and God doesn't want his people to sin.

Similar to when an apostle appeals to the church through the character of God are the times when the apostle, usually Paul, calls on his authority as an apostle of the church. He tells the church his thoughts about what is best.

For instance, in the book of I Corinthians, it appears Paul was answering some questions from the Corinthian church about marriage. In **I Corinthians 7:8-9,** he wrote, *"To the unmarried and the widows I say that it is good for them to remain single as I am. But if they cannot exercise self-control, they should marry. For it is better to marry than to be aflame with passion."* He told the unmarried people that it would be better for their relationship with the

Lord if they remained single, but if they couldn't do that without sinning, they should go ahead and get married. Being married was better than sinning in lust.

What I want you to notice is the way the apostle charged the church. He made only two options available, and he considered one to be better, although he said neither is sinful. Therefore, from that point on the church was bound to two options.

Even today, Christians who seek to obey God abide by these rules. People who possess the gift of singleness can devote their entire lives to the Lord. Most of us, however, end up getting married, because we long to share life with someone and we don't want to sin sexually. The Church embraces both these paths of life, but no others. You cannot live with someone without being married and have the blessing of the Church. When the apostles gave options on a matter, they bound the Church to behavioral standards.

You can be sure that the biblical text applies to you if:

> **1. An apostle instructs his readers to have a certain emotional quality: joy, peace, etc.**
> **2. An apostle appeals to God's character as the basis for his readers' behavior.**
> **3. An apostle appeals to his authority in the church when giving instruction.**

Last, don't forget the common sense, plain reading of the text. Many times an apostle gives a command and doesn't back up his claim with an appeal to the character of God or his authority as an apostle. An example is **Galatians 5:16**: *"But I say, walk by the Spirit and you will not gratify the desires of the flesh."* In these cases, do what he says. Walk by the Spirit. It isn't necessary for the apostle to prove himself to us. Apostles wrote with the authority of God. In general, do what the apostle directs in his letter. If you question a certain command's applicability to us today, seek wise counsel from a trusted, mature Christian or your pastor.

Although the apostles wrote the letters, the real author, who worked through the apostles, was the Holy Spirit, God himself. Simple obedience to the Word of God is worth far more than understanding a complex passage but not carrying out what the Lord wants for your life.

You don't have to be a theologian to understand most of what the apostles tell the church to do in the letters. If you're struggling with a concept that seems to be taught in the epistles but doesn't happen in your church, ask your pastor about it. Evangelical churches and denominations have wrestled long and hard with most of the larger issues that are dealt with in the epistles. Your pastor will not be afraid to answer honest questions from someone earnestly reading the Scriptures to find truth.

Chapter 11

New Testament Prophecy Revelation

When I was a kid, I loved going on family vacations. My parents took us to Disneyland, Yosemite National Park, Hawaii, Canada and Yellowstone National Park, to name a few. I've been privileged with many great memories of family vacations.

My father, however, also owned his own business. Owning your own business is a lot of responsibility. On the day we were supposed to go on vacation, my dad would try to tie up any loose ends that remained at work so that he could spend the week with us. But something always came up. There was always one more client to call or one more deal to close. My dad would do his best to get home as quickly as possible, but we just never knew when that was going to be.

I remember sitting on the stairs in the entryway of our home with my brother and my mom, our bags packed. We waited with breathless anticipation for my father to come bursting in the door and say, "Let's go!" For every vacation the timing was different, and with every vacation, the anticipation never got old.

In a sense, we Christians wait for Jesus in the same way I waited for my father when I was young. Our bags are packed and we are ready to go, but we don't know when he is going to come bursting through the door and say, "Let's go!" I can't wait for that day!

Throughout the history of the Church, many Christians have been misled by a charismatic teacher or preacher to believe that Jesus was coming within a specific time frame. A popular preacher once proclaimed that Jesus was coming back in the year 1984. He misled a lot of people. This is not a new phenomenon. Church history has recorded dozens, if not hundreds of misleading teachers who deluded their followers into believing that Jesus would come back at a certain date or time that had been revealed to only them.

Before we dismiss such thinking, we must remember that this doctrine is so misused precisely because it is our **greatest** hope. Christians desperately want Jesus to come back in their lifetimes, and the New Testament does not discourage such thinking. Many of the greatest Christians in history thought that Jesus was coming back in their lifetimes.

At the end of Revelation, the apostle John records the words of Jesus: *"He who is the faithful witness to all these things says, 'Yes, I am coming soon!'"* Then John adds this exclamation: *"Amen! Come, Lord Jesus!"* **Revelation 22:20**. Nevertheless, the New Testament also cautions against setting a date for the Lord's return. Jesus said, *"No one knows the day or the hour."* **Matthew 24:36**. And in at least one parable, **Matthew 25:14-30**, Jesus hints that the time between his first and Second Coming would be a very long time. In this parable, he compares himself to a land owner who *"went away on a long journey."*

Therefore, in teaching you about New Testament prophecy, I'm not going to concentrate on current events from the newspaper. Many prophecy teachers make a living trying to tie current world events to the events in the New Testament. I'm not going to write about the European Union, or Russian or China. Instead, I'm going to give you some principles that are agreed upon and then allow you to work out your own viewpoint. As the chapter on New Testament history had much in common with the chapter on Old Testament history, so this chapter overlaps in some ways the Old Testament chapter on prophecy. So keep the rules about Old Testament prophecy in mind as we travel through these passages together. Specifically, recall the prophetic principle about the hill and the mountain.

The New Testament clearly teaches that Jesus will come to the earth again. This hope is the focus of an entire chapter in three of the Gospels. Paul spends time on it writing to the church in Thessalonica. Peter encourages his readers with thoughts of the Second Coming. It is the goal and main message of the book of Revelation. It is the end for which the Church, the Bride of Jesus Christ, waits with constant expectation. Since the majority of the prophetic teaching of the New Testament is found in Revelation, we will focus on that book in this section.

Whenever I'm watching a great action movie, it causes me to reflect. The part of the movie I love the most is when the bad guy finally gets what's coming to him. It actually makes me happy! I have a strong sense of justice, so when I watch a movie, I want the bad guy to get justice. I guess that's why I love Revelation. In Revelation, God's patience and grace toward our sinful world and demonic enemies finally comes to an end. It's the culmination of all the biblical prophecy which tells us that God will not abide sin forever, but will someday bring an end to it. So, one thing that you must catch as you read the book of Revelation is that it was written to give hope to all Christians throughout the ages who have longed for God's return to the earth. The good guys win.

While this message is clear in Revelation, it is evident to any thoughtful reader that the book was written in a style not used today. Some scholars call Revelation an example of "apocalyptic" literature which I have already defined for you as "end times" writings. It's a form of literature that went out of style more than 1,500 years ago. Since you probably won't be reading any other apocalyptic books soon, I've compiled a list of things that are important to know as you study Revelation.

1. Everybody has a bias (even me).

Sometimes we fool ourselves into thinking that everybody who doesn't see the world as we do is kind of weird. "If the world would only think like I do, everything would be OK," we think. In our clearer moments we realize that we are just as weird as the next person. It isn't so different with your favorite Bible teacher or writer.

There are a few writers that I really love. I seem to easily soak in everything they write. I find myself simply accepting the things they teach without critically evaluating them. But every once in a while I stop myself and think, "Wait a minute, Matt, do you really agree with EVERYTHING this writer is saying?"

I'm not encouraging you to be overly critical of the pastors and teachers that God has given the body of Christ. Still, it's important to recognize that pastors and Bible teachers are not speaking divine truth when they *interpret* the divine truth. The Bible is God's unique revelation to humanity. Pastors and Bible teachers take that unique revelation and help people understand it. Every pastor I know tries his best to do this faithfully and responsibly. I know that I've agonized over the right interpretation and application of Scripture passages that I preached on. But, for all this, we're still fallible humans. Therefore, we're going to get it wrong from time to time.

This is appropriate to mention as we study Revelation because so many varied interpretations of Revelation exist. Most times, varied interpretations mean somebody is wrong. It doesn't mean they aren't sincerely seeking the true meaning. It means that they have come to the wrong conclusions. Different Bible teachers and pastors have different perspectives on interpreting Revelation. Some authors, the good ones, recognize this and let you know it. Other, less honest authors, try to convince the reader that anyone who doesn't agree with their view of Revelation is wrong. Don't believe it for a second. You may have noticed while reading this book that I point out some of the areas where good Christians disagree. Revelation is one of those. Please don't get caught up in judging what other sincere Christian believers do with the book of Revelation. Do your best to see their point of view (even if you don't agree with it), learn from it, and continue in loving fellowship with them. We all agree that Jesus is coming back. That is what is most important.

If we would only accept that Christians disagree about the book of Revelation we would be fine, but we have trouble understanding and accepting opinions different from ours. Therefore, when reading ANY book on Revelation or Bible prophecy, remember that even if the author doesn't explicitly state what he believes, he most definitely comes from a certain school of thought, even me.

Keep in mind that adopting a certain school of thought or perspective isn't a bad thing. One of the gifts God has given us is the ability to systematize information to make it clearer. There are seminaries and denominations that have systematized the book of Revelation according to the pattern of theology that they believe in, and we can learn a lot from each system. This gift becomes a bad thing only if a teacher claims to know it all and doesn't admit that faithful Christians can have differing perspectives.

As we dive into the book of Revelation, I'm not going to give you a blow-by-blow description of the book. That would mean giving you all the details of my own theological perspective. What I *am* going to give you are some unmistakable signs and symbols that MANY Bible teachers and pastors would agree on — kind of a general overview.

2. Revelation fits the pattern of prophecy found in the Bible.

Revelation begins with an account of what's going on in the seven churches in Asia Minor, **Revelation 2-4**. This is consistent with the nature of a prophetic message. God begins with the local situation and, after addressing the specific churches, broadens the message to discuss his judgment of the entire earth.

Remember the point about the hill and the mountain? **Here it is again**. Jesus begins talking to John about the churches in John's day, but ends with the judgment of the world and the reign of God on the earth. Bigger things are coming.

This must have been very comforting to the people in the specific churches. Many of them were suffering persecution. Jesus lets them know that their suffering will be worth something in the end. In the message to each church, Jesus promises that those who endure will be given specific gifts directly from him in his heavenly kingdom.

We can learn many things from Jesus' message to the seven churches. In many ways, the seven letters function much like the epistle material you learned about earlier. In these seven letters we can see the desire Jesus has for his Church to be pure. It is easy to see that God takes sin in the church very seriously. These letters are also unique because they contain loving encouragement and a critique to the church from Jesus Christ himself. I have sat in silence and humility wondering what Jesus would say to the church I pastor if I were to receive a direct message from him. Since he is the head of the body of Christ, Christians should listen carefully to the words he gives in Revelation to each of the churches.

After the words of Jesus to the churches, John is taken up to heaven and shown things that will take place in the future, **Revelation 4:1**. Notice that the sequence of current situation followed by future situation fits the pattern of biblical prophecy you have already studied about other Biblical prophecy.

3. John receives the information in symbolic form, in pictures he understands. This way God doesn't have to "catch" John up on history, culture, science, military weaponry, etc.

Symbolism can be an effective communication tool. Think about this: The book of Revelation is concerned with Christ's Second Coming and it makes sense for God to communicate to John in symbol forms he understood as opposed to say, showing the entire sequence of events to John as they play out in world history. You and I might want a DVD vision with a news reporter giving a blow-by-blow description of the end times events. Upon further review, though, that might be more difficult than you think.

For an example of what I mean, try it for a second. Imagine going back in time and taking your laptop computer. Let's say your battery has an hour of power left on it and you have just been transported 1,200 years back in time to the Viking culture of northern Europe. Just for kicks, let's say that you could already speak their language, so interpretation is not a problem. Unfortunately, you still have a formidable task. Try explaining to them how your laptop works. It would be **EXTREMELY hard**. You would find yourself trying to explain one thing and then needing to explain something else and so on!

In all probability the people would simply come to the conclusion that your laptop computer was magic sent by the gods. Trying to tell Eric the Red (picture a Viking with a hat with horns on it) that it was an invention powered by electricity that came about through technological advances in electronic calculators in the 1940's using the medium of a TV screen wouldn't get very far!

What if, instead of giving John an exact play-by-play scenario of the end of the world, God used a series of symbols that John was familiar with to depict the main players and events? This seems totally logical to me. Then God wouldn't have to explain all kinds of unnecessary details.

For the sake of argument, let's just say that the Second Coming of Jesus is still about six hundred years from now. (Jesus could come any time, but I'm only doing this to illustrate my point.) I can only imagine that six hundred years from now the human race will possess spaceships, maybe colonies on the moon, colonies under the ocean, advanced transportation systems and weaponry, stuff you see in *Star Trek*, things we can't even conceive of now. Can you imagine God trying to explain that stuff to John? Okay, God is God and he can do anything, but it really taxes the imagination to think about how God would communicate things that far in the future to us humans. Instead, an easier way is to explain the good and the evil players through symbols that John could understand. That way, not only John, but readers in 2008 can appreciate what is being talked about without having to get into the minute details.

So before you get frustrated with some of the symbols in Revelation, think about what could have been the alternative! Revelation is rich with symbols from John's day: large reptiles, candlesticks, trumpets, beasts, bowls that pour out God's judgment on earth, armies on horseback, etc.

4. What the main symbols mean

A) The Number Seven, Revelation 5:1, 8:6

The number seven in Scripture seems to indicate God's perfection or completion. The book of Revelation refers to seven churches. It includes seven angels to the seven churches, seven lamp stands that represent the seven churches, seven seals, seven trumpets, and seven bowls of God's judgment.

Think about what it means to have seven bowls of judgment. The pouring out of the seven bowls of judgment symbolize that God's wrath has been completed and fulfilled. In the book of Genesis, when Pharaoh dreamed about the coming famine, he saw seven fat cows and seven thin cows. God then sent seven years of good crops followed by seven years of famine. When God created the earth, he rested on the seventh day, symbolizing the completion of his work.

In the same way, at the end of the world the number seven indicates God's complete destruction of the wicked and complete salvation of the righteous. Seven signifies God's completed action and the eternal rest that awaits us after his work.

B) The Dragon and the Beast, Revelation 12 and 13

Scripture always depicts Satan as a serpent or a dragon. In the ancient world, a dragon was not the fire-breathing, winged creature we think of. It was simply a large, fierce reptile. So in ancient times, a dragon and a serpent were actually similar. They were unclean, scaly, mean, evil beasts. Satan is portrayed as a serpent in the Garden of Eden and as a dragon at the end of the world.

Revelation 20:2 brings the two symbols of Satan together: *"He seized the dragon, that ancient serpent, who is the devil, or Satan, and bound him for a thousand years."* When the Bible explicitly names the literal figure, in this case, Satan, of a symbolic picture, the Dragon, it's pretty safe to assume that where that symbol is used, the same literal figure is in mind.

Picture This:

**In the book of Revelation,
The Dragon = Satan
The Great Beast = Human Kingdoms of the World**

The beast in Revelation can be thought of as the sum total of human kingdoms and governments. It represents the ultimate human attempt to do away with God and be free of him forever. Revelation is not the first time that God has described human governments as beasts. In Daniel 7, God gave Daniel a vision in which the great kingdoms of the earth were represented by beasts. It happened again in Daniel 8.

In addition to representing the culmination of the world kingdoms, the Beast is also the ruler of the last earthly kingdom, a man who exalts himself directly against God. The Beast is also called the Antichrist because he stands against everything that Jesus stands for. He comes from the kingdoms of this world and also represents them.

C) The Seals, Trumpets and Bowls, Revelation 5 to 16

Something vital to notice in Revelation chapters 5 to 16 is that the seals, trumpets and bowls referred to there may symbolize successive events or they may represent three different ways of explaining similar events. There are good biblical scholars on both sides of this issue. I'll let you wrestle with that concept on your own. I will, however, give you a little help with the symbols themselves and what they stand for.

The Seals – It's Sealed, Then Revealed

In junior high school, when a girl sent me a note telling me she liked me, it was usually folded in such a way that I had to rip it to shreds to get it open. The origami folding techniques of junior high girls has always amazed me!

In ancient times, the way people "encrypted" letters to make sure only the recipients got to read them was by sealing them in wax. They wrote on long sheets of material called papyrus scrolls, then dripped candle wax on the outside edge of the scroll, where it connected to the inner edge of the next roll and immediately stamped the wax with the ring of the sender. That way, if someone broke the seal, the recipient would know that the scroll had already been read. The only person who could rightfully break the seal of a letter was the letter's intended reader.

In Revelation, the seals of God's judgment are so great that no one in all of heaven has the authority to break them and read from the scroll until Jesus, the Lamb of God, shows up. When Jesus comes on the scene, he is recognized as the one who has the authority to execute God's judgment.

The seals represent God's divine will regarding the fate of the earth, and Jesus is the only one who has the authority and the power to break open the seals and read the judgment, since he is God's appointed judge of humanity, **II Timothy 4:1**.

The Trumpets – It's Announced

Before the invention of intercom systems, radios and TV, people announced messages of great importance with loud instruments. In our own country, people rang large, loud bells to announce that a town meeting was imminent or an important event had happened. Long before that, the trumpet was the loudest musical instrument anyone could play. In biblical times, the trumpet signaled both announcements and calls to war.

This imagery is also evident in Revelation. In Revelation, trumpets signal that the time of God's judgment on earth has come. **I Corinthians 15:52** speaks of the "last trumpet" sounding as Jesus gathers all his people from the ends of the earth.

This last trumpet also signals God's final attack on the people who refuse to worship him. As God's army descends from heaven, a trumpet blast signals the coming event. This final trumpet announcement signals great relief and joy for God's people but great horror for those who have rejected Jesus as Lord.

The Bowls – It's Poured Out

Then I heard a loud voice from the temple saying to the seven angels, "Go, pour out the seven bowls of God's wrath on the earth" **Revelation 16:1**.

The seven bowls in Revelation symbolize that God's wrath has reached its limit. They indicate that the time has come to pour out what has been stored up for so long.

God is patient and loving; He doesn't want anyone to perish, but he also doesn't overlook sin. The Bible talks about the wicked storing up for themselves wrath on the day when God will reveal himself to the earth. *"But because of your stubbornness and your unrepentant heart, you are storing up wrath against yourself for the day of God's wrath, when his righteous judgment will be revealed"* **Romans 2:5**.

John's vision of bowls is also consistent with the way God revealed his judgment to the Israelites in the Old Testament. Consider **Isaiah 51:22**: *"Thus says your Lord, the LORD, your God who pleads the cause of his people: 'Behold, I have taken from your hand the cup of staggering; the bowl of my wrath you shall drink no more.'"* God called his judgment a "bowl of wrath" as he does in Revelation.

D) The Great Prostitute and Babylon, Revelation 17-18,

Revelation 17:5 ties the great prostitute and Babylon together: *"A mysterious name was written on her* (the prostitute's) *forehead: "Babylon the Great, Mother of all Prostitutes and Obscenities in the World."* parenthesis mine. In the New Testament, Babylon is a code name for Rome. *"She who is in Babylon, chosen together with you, sends you her greetings, and so does my son Mark"* **I Peter 5:13**. Peter never went to Babylon so far as any historical record shows. Peter did go to Rome though, and so did his disciple, John Mark, who eventually wrote the Gospel of Mark. Perhaps the early Christians used Babylon as a code word for Rome because they were afraid their documents would be intercepted by the Roman authorities. We'll probably never know for sure.

Because we know that Babylon was code for Rome, we can be fairly certain that the reference to Babylon being "surrounded by seven hills" in **Revelation 17:9** means Rome. The ancient city of Rome was surrounded by seven hills. These clues are what lead biblical scholars to their conclusions.

Through the years, this reference to Rome has led many prominent church leaders from various backgrounds to view the great enemy of the Lord as the Roman Catholic Church. The seat of power for the Catholic Church has always been Rome, where the Pope resides. For some theologians, it's an easy step to say that some future Pope will be the Antichrist. While I am a Protestant pastor and I disagree with many of the teachings and beliefs of the Roman Catholic Church, I need to issue a word of warning here. Speculating about prophecy can be dangerous. The fact is nobody knows who the Antichrist will be. He will be revealed during earth's last days, and we can't just pin the tail on the Roman Catholic Church because we like the target. I believe God has given us the clues we will need for that time in **II Thessalonians 2:1-11**. Until then, we shouldn't waste time trying to unveil something that will remain hidden until its fulfillment.

E) The New Jerusalem, Revelation 21-22

The City of God, the New Jerusalem, plays a prominent role in the later chapters of Revelation. It will be the final residence of all the righteous people who have ever lived. God will no longer separate himself from us. God began this with Jesus. In Jesus, God came to earth as a man and lived with us. Then, at Jesus' request, the Father sent the Holy Spirit to indwell and seal all Christians during the Church age. The final consummation and gathering of believers will be even greater. God will come to earth with his entire eternal kingdom and will set up shop to live with us and rule over the creation.

I saw the Holy City, the New Jerusalem, coming down out of heaven from God, prepared as a bride beautifully dressed for her husband. And I heard a loud voice from the throne saying, "Now the dwelling of God is with men, and he will live with them. They will be his people, and God himself will be with them and be their God. He will wipe every tear from their eyes. There will be no more death or mourning or

crying or pain, for the old order of things has passed away"
Revelation 21:2-4

The New Jerusalem is God's sign to us that everything will be better in the end. Jesus wins and we live happily ever after. Once the Enemy is finally destroyed, God has wonderful things in store for us.

God's kingdom will replace human "beasts" — man-made kingdoms. Human kingdoms are full of sin and will be destroyed, but God's kingdom is full of righteousness and will last forever. In Revelation, God wipes the earth clean of all sin and death and comes to live with his chosen people forever.

Revelation contains some disturbing images and troubling concepts, but you should never forget that the ultimate message of Revelation is that God conquers Satan, sin and death finally and fully. The victory of Jesus on the cross began the defeat of the enemy. When Jesus died on the cross, he crushed the head of Satan. At the end of time, when God destroys sin and death and casts Satan into the lake of fire, all the enemies of Christ will be forever obliterated. **Revelation 22:3** reads: *"No longer will there be anything accursed, but the throne of God and of the Lamb will be in it, and his servants will worship him."* Always remember that the main message of Revelation is "Jesus wins!"

Chapter 12

God's Word as Your Daily Spiritual Guide

"God, who has called you into <u>fellowship</u> with his Son Jesus Christ our Lord, is faithful." **I Corinthians 1:9**

The Oxford Universal Dictionary defines fellowship as: *"Partnership, community of interest, companionship, company. Communion, the spirit of comradeship."*

Nothing is more vital to our spiritual well-being than a close, intimate walk with God our Father through Jesus Christ. So far in this book, I've outlined what I, as a pastor and Bible teacher, believe are correct practices to help you in your reading and understanding of the Bible. It is possible, however, to correctly read and understand Scripture and not be very close to God himself.

The point of the Scriptures is to get us to Jesus, God's glorious son, and through Jesus, to have a relationship with God as our Father. In fact, Jesus came and died for our sins to give us fellowship with the Father. *"We proclaim to you what we have seen and heard, so that you also may have fellowship with us. And our fellowship is with the Father and with his Son, Jesus Christ"* **I John 1:3**.

This fellowship includes many benefits for us: free and unhindered access to God's throne through prayer, security knowing that when we die, we will be safe in heaven with the Father, peace through all life circumstances, knowing that God is working in us for our ultimate good, **Romans 8:28**. I could go on and on listing the benefits of fellowship with God. To sum them all up, you may think of fellowship with God as *close friendship*. Jesus said, "*You are my friends if you do what I command you*" **John 15:14**. Therefore, if you have become a follower of Jesus, you are his friend.

Fellowship Means Daily Communication with God

The chief way that many Christians throughout the ages have fostered this fellowship, or friendship, with God is through a personal, daily, and private time with God. Some Christians call this time their **personal devotions**. Personal devotions usually consist of reading the Bible and spending time in prayer on your own. One of the best ways for this to take place regularly in your life is to set aside time every single day for developing these habits as a means of intimacy with God. When Jesus was on earth, he slipped away for regular times of quiet prayer with the Father. Read the following verses and allow Jesus' example to sink into your heart.

> **Mark 1:35-37** – *Very early in the morning, while it was still dark, Jesus got up, left the house and went off to a solitary place, where he prayed. Simon and his companions went to look for him, and when they found him, they exclaimed: "Everyone is looking for you."*

> **Luke 6:12** – *One of those days, Jesus went out to a mountainside to pray, and spent the night praying to God. When morning came, he called his disciples to him and chose twelve of them.*

> **Matthew 14:22-24** – *Immediately Jesus made the disciples get into the boat and go on ahead of him to the other side, while he dismissed the crowd. After he had dismissed them, he went up on a mountainside by himself to pray. When evening came, he was there alone.*

Luke 22:41 – *He withdrew about a stone's throw beyond them, knelt down and prayed.*

Jesus placed a high priority on his own relationship with the Father. The demands on his time and energy would overwhelm any of us. He constantly re-energized himself through times of prayer alone with the Father. On occasion he had to rise before the sun came up to get away from the demands on him and meet with the Father.

I can't stress enough that too many Christians live at the frantic pace of the modern world without taking any real time to spend with the Lord in prayer. We have cell phones, e-mail, text messaging, video conferencing, more ways to communicate than ever, yet many Christians miss the regular practice of instant access to the throne of God through regular prayer.

Four years ago I was blessed to plant a church in Southern California. I had been in ministry for many years, but this was the first time I was the senior pastor of a congregation. I've found myself more drawn to prayer because of the greater responsibility, and I can tell you that I actually feel the pull to prayer stronger and stronger the longer I pastor a church. Prayer is the real work of God's people.

Consider Jesus' Dependence on Scripture

In addition to prayer, Jesus showed a thorough grasp of Scripture and constantly used it to minister to others and to rebuke the enemy. In Jesus' time, the Old Testament scrolls were too valuable for everyone to possess. In fact, usually only the synagogues had copies, so people memorized large chunks of God's Word.

We see this is true of Jesus in the following examples. In **Matthew 4:4** Jesus quoted from **Deuteronomy 8:3**: *"Jesus answered, 'Man does not live on bread alone, but on every word that comes from the mouth of God.'"* Jesus was saying that God's Word is as important to our souls as physical bread is to our bodies.

Did you know that when Jesus was tempted in the desert by the Devil, all of his responses came straight from Scripture, and more specifically, from the book of Deuteronomy! Go, Jesus! He defeated Satan using only one Old Testament book. Jesus is incredible!

Later, when the religious teachers misquoted and misapplied Scripture for their sinful purposes, Jesus again directed them to Scripture to correct their faulty understanding. *"They said, 'Moses permitted a man to write a certificate of divorce and send her away.' 'It was because your hearts were hard that Moses wrote you this law,' Jesus replied. 'But at the beginning of creation God "made them male and female." For this reason a man will leave his father and mother and be united to his wife, and the two will "become one flesh." So they are no longer two, but one. Therefore what God has joined together, let not man separate.'"* **Mark 10: 4-7**. Jesus quoted from **Genesis 1:27** to answer the Pharisees' incorrect interpretation.

Some time later, when Jesus had risen from the grave, two of his disciples were on the road to Emmaus and Jesus convinced them from the Scriptures that the Messiah had to suffer, *"And beginning with Moses and all the Prophets, he explained to them what was said in all the Scriptures concerning himself"* **Luke 24:27.**

Jesus had a thorough knowledge of Scripture because in the Scriptures God reveals himself to us. We come to know what he is like and what he wants for us. Therefore, the Scriptures were never far from Jesus' conversations.

More Reasons to Make Daily Devotions Your Top Priority

If this brief survey of Jesus' way of life doesn't convince you of the importance of spending time everyday in prayer and God's Word, think about the example of the early church from **Acts 2:42**: *"They devoted themselves to the apostles' teaching and to the fellowship, to the breaking of bread and to prayer."* The early church devoted themselves to four things: the apostles' teaching, which is what we now have as the New Testament, the fellowship, the breaking of bread and prayer.

I encourage you to look up the following Bible passages that emphasize the importance of the Scriptures and prayer for our daily lives.

Prayer
Ephesians 6:18
Philippians 4:6
I Thessalonians 5:17
I Timothy 2:8
James 5:13
Scripture
Hebrews 4:12
James 1:21-22
I Peter 2:2
Ephesians 6:17

Finally, take note of the importance Paul places on the Word of God and prayer in **Ephesians 6:17-18**: *"Take the helmet of salvation and the sword of the Spirit, which is the <u>word of God</u>. And <u>pray in the Spirit on all occasions</u> with all kinds of prayers and requests. With this in mind, be alert and always keep on praying for all the saints."*

Now that you know the priority that prayer and the Scriptures should have in the life of the believer, let's look at *how* best to apply those activities to your daily time with the Lord.

Speaking to God – Prayer

There is nothing magical about prayer. It's simply talking to God who has become our Father through Jesus Christ. We need to communicate with those we love. If I only talked to my wife for five minutes every other day, she would think something was wrong with our marriage, and she would be right. But many Christians want to feel closer to God without spending the necessary time talking with him. It isn't going to happen.

There's no magic pill where someone gets close to God without walking those paths that make one person closer to another in any relationship. *If you don't spend time with God, you aren't going to get closer to him.* If you do take the time to spend with him, speaking to him and listening to him, you will reap the rewards.

Prayer doesn't have to be long, drawn out and boring. Look at the prayer in John 11 that Jesus prayed before he raised Lazarus from the dead. He began by saying, *"Father, I thank you that you always hear me..."* It isn't a long, majestic approach, but a son coming before his Father, thanking him for always listening.

Prayer shouldn't be irreverent or disrespectful to God, but the fact of the matter is that most people don't pray like they talk. It isn't right that we talk to our Father in a way that is unlike our normal method of communication. Talk to God as you talk to a friend or loved one, conversationally. The Bible tells us, *"So let us come boldly to the throne of our gracious God. There we will receive his mercy, and we will find grace to help us when we need it"* **Hebrews 4:16**.

Although God does speak to his children in prayer, for the most part the purpose of prayer is to lift our praises and requests to God. A familiar model called ACTS has helped many Christians make their prayer time focused and productive. ACTS stands for Adoration, Confession, Thanksgiving, and Supplication. As we pray, ACTS helps us remember that prayer is more than just asking God for things, it is praising him for who he is and thanking him for what he has done in our lives.

On many mornings, as I begin my prayer time, the Lord prompts me to just praise him. Other times, I am so affected by a certain need that I spend the entire time praying to him about just that one thing. Therefore, the ACTS guideline is just that: a guide to help you remember the different aspects of prayer. The Holy Spirit will direct you as you pray. Remember to be sensitive to the Holy Spirit's direction as you pray.

Did You Know?

> **You only grow in a relationship with those people you spend time with. It's no different in your relationship with God. If you don't spend time with him, you won't grow.**

When you commit to regular and honest communication with God, something else must come along with it — privacy. I think of my relationship with my wife. We have three beautiful children, but sometimes we need to go away from their presence and just talk. Sometimes we like to be alone in a quiet restaurant so that we can communicate without any distractions.

The closer you are with someone, the more you enjoy uninterrupted conversation with them. Jesus says, *"But when you pray, go into your room and shut the door and pray to your Father who is in secret. And your Father who sees in secret will reward you"* **Matthew 6:6.**

Prayer is an essential component to growing as a Christian. Therefore, commit to regular, honest, respectful and private conversation with the Lord. Do whatever you have to do to fit it into your schedule. Write it on your daily calendar, your blackberry, or your refrigerator planner. Don't start off trying to go from no time in prayer to an hour. Instead, gradually increase your time. Or, if you have not been praying, commit to just ten minutes a day during the first week. Once you master that, increase your time with him.

Listening to God – Scripture

I know of no better way to become familiar with Scripture or with the character of God than to go systematically verse by verse, chapter by chapter, through God's Word.

If you are a new Christian, it is helpful to start with a New Testament Gospel: Matthew, Mark, Luke or John. Once you read a Gospel, you should progress to one of the epistles, such as I John, Ephesians, Philippians, etc.

Some Christians start at the beginning of the Bible, in the book of Genesis. Most people who do this don't get past the books of Moses, the first five books of the Bible. I encourage any new Christian to begin with a Gospel or a simple epistle, like I John. Don't try and conquer too much at one time. Read a chapter a day. Remember, as with prayer, don't try and conquer the whole world in a day. Simply begin to be regular and consistent in your approach and see that the Lord does.

For those who may be looking for a way to glean more insight from their daily reading of the Bible, my wife once wrote a brief, easy-to-understand guide to beginning your daily devotions that I have included below in italics. Her version is for those who want to slow down with a certain section of scripture and really dig into what it means.

*As with any opportunity to study the Word of God, **approach it with prayer**, asking the Holy Spirit to guide you. There are no limits to what the Lord can do when you sit with him and open the Scriptures. The purpose of this study will be to go through the Scriptures **slowly and carefully**.*

*First, get a notebook or journal; a simple one will do. Start in the New Testament, preferably the book of **I John**. Read one verse at a time, and use one page per verse, leaving plenty of room for yourself to write as much as you need. Do a few verses each day. With each verse you read, follow this pattern:*

A. *Write the entire verse in your notebook.*
B. *Restate the verse in your own words.*
C. *Now, write your insights and application of the verse, either at a general or a personal level. This is the part of the study where the Holy Spirit teaches and ministers to you personally. Don't rush through this. Repeat the verse to yourself if necessary. Ask God to reveal the meaning to you so that you can apply it to your life.*

It's always fun to round out your devotional time with a reading in the Old Testament and poetry from the Psalms or Proverbs as well. If you are currently working your way through a New Testament book, then add to your reading the following:

• *Each day, read at least one chapter in the Old Testament Doing this will familiarize you with the flow of the Old Testament as well as allow you to dive into its richness. Reading the Old Testament often leaves you wanting to come back to get the rest of the story!*

- *Read the chapter in Proverbs that corresponds to each day of the month. (On the 1ˢᵗ of the month, read ch.1 and so on),* **or**
- *Read a Psalm a day (praise, worship, prayer, repentance, victory, prophecy – it's all in there!)*

Beginning a daily devotional time with your Lord and Savior is life-changing. Just remember that **the goal is to be consistent.** Making new habits takes time, but it can become as easy as brushing your teeth!

Some Christians focus on the amount they can read in a sitting; I don't recommend that practice. Quality is much better than quantity. It's better to read and write about five verses that you will be able to comprehend and remember throughout the day than five chapters that you forget very quickly.

As you begin to consistently read the Bible, you will begin to ask questions of the text. That is a great thing. Keep a notebook handy to write your questions down. Sometimes the text itself will answer your questions in a few verses. Other times you may need to save your question and ask a mature Christian. Either way, you are learning more about the Bible as you read, ask questions and understand.

One of the best things about reading the Bible is that it never grows old. In my journey of reading the Bible daily, I've found that although I have read a passage of Scripture perhaps twenty times, God continues to give me new insight into the passage.

Do you know why this happens? It's because God's Word is alive and active. **Hebrews 4:12** says, *"For the word of God is **living and active**, sharper than any two-edged sword, piercing to the division of soul and of spirit, of joints and of marrow, and discerning the thoughts and intentions of the heart."*

Scripture doesn't change, but I grow and change in my relationship with God. The Holy Spirit convicts me in new ways about my sin. He encourages me in new ways about my relationship with the Father. He challenges me each time I read.

In fact, the book that I have read the most, Proverbs, continually amazes me in its ability to bring new things to my attention. During certain years of my life, I've read through the book of Proverbs from beginning to end each month. So in any given year, I read that book of the Bible twelve times, and yet, I can't wait to get into it each day to see what it holds. God is amazing. His ability to write something that we can read over and over but gain new insight each time is incredible.

Another important reason to continually read the Bible is that it allows God to infect and affect your daily life. I cannot tell you how many times in my walk with Jesus, something I have read in the Scriptures that morning directly applied to a situation that I was dealing with. It's miraculous. It is God stepping in and allowing the pattern of my daily reading to interact with the problems and circumstances that I face on a regular basis.

In addition to this, the more I know the Bible, the more I can share it with others. If I am not reading my Bible, I may be able to give my own counsel, or some wise advice I have heard, but I have found that the Scriptures minister to people in a way that my wisdom cannot. When I can share a Scripture verse with someone, I am pointing them to God and his Word, not me. They go home and look up the Scripture and are comforted by God himself instead of some words that I have given them on my own.

Recording Your Walk – Journaling

In addition to prayer and reading the Bible, I have added the element of journaling to the daily plan of spending time with God. Writing down what God is doing in our lives is a sure way to remember it. As we journal, we record our walk with God in a way we can read about later. This makes us less prone to forget what God is teaching us. Although most ancient people couldn't journal, most modern people can. Many of the great devotional writers of Christian history are known to us primarily through their journals.

The three components of daily devotions: prayer, Scripture reading and journaling have made up a significant part of the daily walk of many godly Christians throughout the years. Some of the most popular and classic devotional books have come from

Christians who simply took the time to record what God was doing in their lives through their prayers and Scripture reading.

In the classic devotional, *My Utmost for His Highest*, Oswald Chambers wrote down his thoughts as he spent time with God in silent prayer and reading. His devotional is a worldwide bestseller.

As an aside, devotional writings should by no means replace our own Bible reading. Some Christians fall into the habit of reading other people's devotional writings as their own devotions. I am sure the author of the devotional book would not approve of that practice. Reading other Christians' devotional writing is great to do, but it should *never* replace your own daily reading of the Word of God.

I recommend that as you pray and read the Scriptures, you keep a journal or notebook handy to jot down the thoughts, encouragements and convictions that the Lord brings to your mind. A journal allows you to keep track of prayer requests and answers to prayer that God has given you, as well as record your thoughts about Scripture as you systematically read through books of the Bible.

Keeping a record of the prayers that God has answered is a wonderful way to record what God has done in your life. If God is real, then he is going to answer prayer. Sometimes I get discouraged because I'm focusing on myself or my problems, but when I take the time to look through all the prayers that God has answered, it immediately encourages me. We must remember what God has done in our lives.

My wife keeps a journal of answered prayers and, at the writing of this chapter, she has recorded more than eight hundred specific answers to prayer in the past fifteen years. That's right, eight hundred! We all have a tendency to forget what God has done in our lives, but if we take the time to write it down, we can recall it.

Additionally, when I write down my thoughts on a Scripture passage, I am relearning what I have just read. Journaling helps me concentrate on the passage I'm reading instead of just reading it to get through it and on with my day.

Scheduling Time with God

Once you recognize the importance of having daily time with God, you need to make it a regular part of your day. Let's think about the best time of day for you to pray and read God's Word.

In his book, *Spiritual Leadership*, Oswald Sanders points out that many Christian leaders of past ages followed Jesus' example in **Mark 1: 35-37** and rose early in the morning to spend time alone with the Father. The father of the Protestant Reformation, Martin Luther, once said about a busy day, *"Work, work from early till late. In fact, I have so much to do that I shall spend the first three hours in prayer."*

Notice how different that is from many of us. If we have a busy day, one of the first things that we put on the shelf is our personal time with God. Yet to Martin Luther, the busier his day, the more prayer that day required. What an upside down approach to time management. What a Christ-like model.

A common response is "But you don't know how busy I am." I don't pretend to know how busy anybody else is, but I do know that any day spent without time seeking to know more about God through his Word and prayer is simply too busy, period.

Some Christians have the habit of reading the Scriptures and praying at night before they go to bed. Whenever you take time to spend with God is good, but let me suggest that morning is the most appropriate time for us to be with the Father. If we wait until night-time to read the Bible, we have lost the opportunity to allow God's Word to affect us for that day. To make things even worse, we are about to spend approximately eight hours in unconscious sleep so that when we wake up, we begin a new day with little thought of the day before. The Word may sanctify our dreams, which we do need, yet the opportunity to fill our minds with God's Word in the morning, before we start our day, should be taken by all who can possibly manage it. David said in the **Psalm 119:147**, *"I rise up before dawn and cry for help; I have put my hope in your word."*

Another reason why the morning is an optimum time for prayer is that it is usually silent in the early morning. When it is quiet, it is easier for us to concentrate on our prayer time.

My encouragement to spend time with God in the morning is not an ironclad principle. It is, however, a suggestion that has been put into practice by many Christian saints through the years that has yielded much fruit. The Word of God and prayer are able to inform our entire day when we literally "seek first his kingdom" in the priority of our day.

Why It's Important to Not Just Read — But to *Memorize* Scripture

Now that we have the wonderful opportunity to have our own personal copy of the Scriptures, it would be a waste for us not to regularly memorize and dive into the depths of the Word for refreshment and encouragement. If they were such an important aspect of Jesus' life and ministry, shouldn't they be for us?

Some of you may be thinking, "Well, maybe so, but Jesus had this world-changing ministry to accomplish, and I'm just a regular person, so it can't be as important for me to know the Scriptures like Jesus did." Consider this: although Jesus was fully human, Jesus did not possess a sin nature. He never sinned and never felt the urge to sin from the *inside* of his being. He was always challenged and tempted to do evil from outside of himself.

We, however, do possess a sin nature; the desire to sin tempts us from inside ourselves. We're tempted from the inside *and* from the outside. Therefore, we need Scripture MORE than Jesus did. Although he had a world-changing ministry to perform, his inner nature was totally in line with the path that the Father laid out for his life.

Our inner natures sometimes fight against the things that God has for us because we still struggle with our internal desire to sin. That's why it is all the more important to have the Word of God residing in our hearts, ready to be used against outward temptation, as Jesus modeled for us, and inward temptation, which we all struggle with.

Many people today really believe that they could never memorize large portions of scripture. However, they can remember the lyrics to every popular song in the last twenty years! Sometimes I laugh to myself when I hear just one line from an old song on the radio. (By old, I mean 1980s.) All I have to hear is one line and I can recite the lyrics of the entire song. I may not have heard the song in decades, but it all comes right back to me.

I don't know about you, but I have no excuse for not memorizing Scripture. If I can remember the lyrics to an old rap song by LL Cool J, I think God can help me memorize Scripture! And God can help me to get rid of the LL Cool J song!

Our Purpose and Motivation for Having Devotions

If we "do" our devotions just to be done with them, we lose the spiritual benefit. Our devotional time is to help us, not get God's approval. He loves us with an everlasting love that cannot be fathomed. Our devotions provide an avenue for *our* growth in the grace and knowledge of the Lord Jesus. You will get out of your devotions what you put into them.

Daily devotions are not a trophy to make you spiritually superior to other Christians. If your motive for devotions is pride or anything other than a desire to grow closer to God, you will fail badly. The practice of daily prayer, Scripture reading and journaling has one end: **to grow closer to God the Father and Jesus Christ our Lord.**

If you enter into it with that purpose, you will find that God's promises are true. David wrote, *"The Lord is near to all those that call on him, who call on him in truth"* **Psalms 145:18**.

The practice of reading, journaling and praying get us ready to live life in God's kingdom. God has an incredible world of peace, joy and fulfilling work for all those who make themselves ready to be used.

Regular devotions have changed millions of Christians through the ages and they could change you. Take time for this important area of your Christian walk. You will not be disappointed.

Conclusion

Okay, you've learned a fair amount about ancient culture. You're gaining an eye to see key details in the biblical text. You're remembering that the context of a Bible passage usually gives the best clues to the meaning of that passage. You've learned that a passage cannot mean what it never meant to the original audience.

Now what? Well, get at it! Go study your Bible. Read portions of Scripture that you haven't read before. If you think you have the gift of teaching, ask your pastor for opportunities to teach and learn to accurately handle the Word of God.

The best part of learning how to interpret the Bible is to use that skill to interpret the Bible. One of the best benefits is teaching others how to do the same. That's why I wrote this book. It's one of the joys of my life to help someone discover how to use God's Word accurately. The great news is that you can do it, too.

This book has provided you with a basic framework for studying the Bible. You can find other engaging books, Bible dictionaries, encyclopedias, and additional resources out there to help you interpret and teach God's Word. You can also ask your pastor, check out your church library, go to a Christian bookstore or look online to find them. This book and all those resources are great tools, but none of them even comes close to the Word itself.

Get into God's Word! I encourage you to continue your quest to be a faithful disciple of Jesus by accurately handling the Word he has given to us. May God bless you as you begin to *read the Word*!

Appendix

Who Decided Which Books to Include in the Bible?

When I was young, my friends and I made our ultimate all-star teams from our baseball card collections. We'd spend hours laboring over which players to include on our teams.

When we were finished, we'd compare and contrast each team, endlessly picking over the finer points of each player's batting averages and home runs. We were only eleven years old, but it was serious business to us.

Of course, the selections we made involved some interpretive decisions on our part. There was always room to criticize each others' decisions because we all came from a biased viewpoint. I don't think any of us ever completely agreed on anything.

When it comes to the Bible, how did the Church, with so many leaders, ever agree on the sixty-six books that would make up what we consider the Old and New Testaments? In addition to teaching you how to read each section of Scripture, I wanted to give you the background on how the books of the Bible came together in the first place.

Ultimately, the books in the Bible are there because God directly inspired them. He directed and guided their writing to such a degree that the men who wrote them were writing from their own perspectives but writing timeless and divine truth. How that happened is still somewhat of a mystery. We do know that the Holy Spirit led the authors of scripture as they wrote. **I Peter 1:21**

However, from a human perspective, how did the Bible get put together and who decided it should be the books we have today? Can you be sure that the books you have in your Bible today are really the ones that are supposed to be there? To answer that question, we must go back to the beginning of Christianity — actually, to the one who began it.

Christianity began with Jesus, and Jesus was a Jew. Jesus believed in the Scriptures of the Jewish nation, which we now call the Old Testament. Jesus taught from the Old Testament and considered it the supreme guide for life. He said in **Matthew 5:17-18**, *"Do not think that I have come to abolish the Law or the Prophets; I have not come to abolish them but to fulfill them. For truly, I say to you, until heaven and earth pass away, not an iota, not a dot, will pass from the Law until all is accomplished."*

In his day and age, the Jewish Bible was known as "The Law and the Prophets." When Jesus said that he came to fulfill the Law and the Prophets, he didn't question their origin. He knew they were from God.

Whenever Jesus talked about the Old Testament, it was with the utmost reverence. Therefore, because of Jesus' high view of the Old Testament Scriptures, the apostles continued to use the Old Testament when teaching about Jesus. To them, it was a given that the Old Testament was God's Word.

For the first ten years of the Church, all early Christians were Jews. They already believed and revered the Old Testament as Scripture. They believed that the Old Testament Scriptures spoke about Jesus and spent their time convincing other Jews of this. The book of Acts contains many examples of Paul going into Jewish synagogues and preaching Jesus as the Christ, using the Old Testament Scriptures.

"Paul and Silas...came to Thessalonica, where there was a Jewish synagogue. As was Paul's custom, he went to the synagogue service, and for three Sabbaths in a row he used the Scriptures to reason with the people. He explained the prophecies and proved that the Messiah must suffer and rise from the dead. He said, "This Jesus I'm telling you about is the Messiah." **Acts 17:1-3**

I could cite many other Scriptures as well but I think you get the point. The early Christian church used the same "Bible" as the Jews. We now call it the Old Testament.

The real question is, "how did they come up with the belief that certain books should be placed alongside the Old Testament Scriptures to form a new portion of the Bible?" In studying Church history, it seems that the early church had one main test that a book had to meet before they considered it worthy of being Scripture. Was the book written by an apostle or a close friend of the apostles? Along with this one test, they had some rational criteria for whether it should be included or not. These can be stated as:

---

1. The Test - Was it written by an apostle or close associate of an apostle?
2. Rational Criteria - Is it accepted by the whole Church?
3. Rational Criteria - Is it consistent with the Old Testament and other New Testament Scripture?
4. Rational Criteria - Does it have the "feel" of Scripture?

Let's briefly examine these four questions and why the early Church asked them.

1. Was it written by an apostle or a close associate?

It was important to the early Church to keep a record of the teachings of the apostles. It was vital that the Church have a direct link to Jesus. If a book was being considered for Scripture, it had to have been written by an apostle or someone in their circle of friendship and influence.

The apostles Peter, John, Matthew, and Paul account for twenty one of the twenty seven New Testament books. James and Jude, the brothers of Jesus, account for two books. Luke and Mark, friends of the apostles, account for three and the book of Hebrews, whose authorship is debated, rounds out the list of books. Even in Hebrews, there is evidence that the author, whoever he was, was close to the original followers of Christ. *"I want you to know that our brother* ***Timothy*** *has been released from jail. If he comes here soon, I will bring him with me to see you.* **Hebrews 13:23.** This verse shows that the author of Hebrews was a friend of Timothy, who was a close friend of Paul. All the authors of the New Testament pass the test of either being an apostle or being well within the sphere of the apostle's friendship.

For instance, Church history records that the Gospel of Mark was written by John Mark as he followed and wrote down the sermons of the apostle Peter. Peter called Mark "my son" in **I Peter 5:13**, so we know that Peter and Mark had a close relationship. Although an apostle didn't write Mark, someone close to an apostle did.

Another example is the book of Acts, which was written by Luke. He was not an apostle, but was a traveling companion of the apostle Paul. In the later chapters of Acts, the travel log of Paul and his companions switches from a "they" voice to a "we" voice, as in "we traveled to such and such a place." Luke was with Paul on some of his journeys, which provides evidence that Paul approved of Luke's writings. In addition to this, Paul mentioned Luke as one of his companions in chapter four of Colossians.

While Christians wrote many commendable documents in the years after the Church started, the only ones that made it into Scripture were those written by apostles or close associates of the apostles.

2. Is it accepted by the <u>Church</u>?

The reason I underlined the word Church is because I'm not referring to one church or a group of churches in an area, but to the leaders of the entire Church in the Mediterranean world.

The leaders of the Church did get together and talk. They also wrote letters to one another. It was a foregone conclusion that something was Scripture only if the entire Church recognized a certain book's importance.

Certain books had an appeal to a group of churches in a certain area, but only the books that everybody knew about made it into Scripture. It's not just that a certain book was more popular or appeared on a first-century version of the *New York Times* bestseller list. Rather, *it needed to be both well known and highly valued by the Church.*

Remember, there were only twelve original apostles. When Paul or John wrote a letter to a church, it was so important that that church did everything it could to get that letter reproduced and into the hands of the other churches. In **Colossians 4:15-16**, Paul wrote, *"Give my greetings to the brothers at Laodicea, and to Nympha and the church in her house. <u>After this letter has been read to you, see that it is also read in the church of the Laodiceans and that you in turn read the letter from Laodicea.</u>"*

From the earliest times, Christians have been voracious copiers of Scripture. This may not seem amazing in our day of Christian bookstores and twenty different Bible translations, but it was extremely important before the invention of the printing press and in a culture in which Christians were persecuted. I once read that the English word *traitor* comes from a word meaning "hander over," referring to Christians who handed over copies of the Scriptures to the Roman authorities who arrested them for their faith. The early Christians were intensely committed to the Scriptures.

Also, the church was not divided into Catholic, Protestant and various other denominations until hundreds of years after the apostles died. Therefore, the unity of the bishops or pastors of the churches was more important than it might seem today.

The early Church comprised people from places as diverse as Rome, Italy and Alexandria, North Africa. A book was confirmed as Scripture only when it had a majority of support from a wide spectrum of the Church. When they all agreed about something, it was significant.

3. Is it consistent with the Old Testament and other New Testament Scripture?

The document in question had to line up with the other Scriptures already accepted by the Church. If a book or letter contradicted the teaching of Jesus or the record of the Old Testament, it was not considered Scripture.

When you read the book of Romans, you see that Paul had a firm grasp of the Old Testament law and its relationship to our hearts. Paul accurately described the role and purpose of the Old Testament law as seen through the sacrifice of Jesus on the Cross.

Acts 7 records a long sermon from the deacon Stephen, in which he accurately recounts Israel's history and comes to the same conclusions as Jesus did in **Matthew 23:29-36**. Stephen's speech is consistent with both the Old Testament and with Jesus' words about the current leaders of Israel.

Hebrews 11 lists what many consider to be the "hall of faith" of Old Testament heroes. It accurately describes the lives of such people as Abraham, Moses, etc.

All the books called Scripture by the early Church had an accurate view of the Old Testament Scriptures and the teaching of Jesus. This point is important because the early Church leaders faced constant opposition from the Jewish leaders. They needed to prove that Jesus and the Church he started correctly interpreted the Old Testament Scriptures about the Messiah.

4. Does it have the "feel" of Scripture?

Early Christians spent hours committing the Scriptures to memory. They could tell the difference between profound writing and something that was not.

You do essentially the same thing when you distinguish great fiction from dime store fiction. Early Christians were better at it because the leaders of the Church read Scripture ALL the time and they regularly read, OUT LOUD, entire portions of the Bible to their congregations. A lot of people back then couldn't read, and they didn't have their own Bibles at home anyway. If they wanted to remember something about Scripture, they had to memorize it.

The early Church leaders spent their lives, their time, their energy and their intellects devouring Scripture. Even most pastors today don't have the memory for Scripture that those men had. The early Church leaders didn't have five hundred other books on ministry in their personal libraries. Before the printing press made the printed word widely available, everything had to be copied by hand. Parchments were expensive and time-consuming to produce, so the only books in their care were usually Scripture or writings from the previous bishop of their church.

Consequently, when they read a fake letter or even good Christian teaching, they could usually tell right away that it wasn't the same as the holy Bible, inspired by God. A good example is the letter to the Corinthians from Clement of Rome, (not the books of I & II Corinthians written by Paul). Clement was an early church leader but his letter to the Corinthian church did not pass the tests, or criteria, of being divinely inspired scripture. Historians believe the author was the same Clement mentioned by Paul in **Philippians 4:3**, and his letter was read in some early churches, but it never gained the status of Scripture precisely because it isn't Scripture. It was not divinely inspired and it didn't pass the four tests. Therefore, even though it's good reading, it isn't contained in the collection of inspired literature, our Bible. The bishops who read it over and over came to the conclusion that it didn't have the feel of Scripture, and they were right.

In conclusion, it is better to say that the early Church discovered which books should be counted as Scripture rather than that they decided upon Scripture. There was never a group of people who came together and said, "Let's make these books our sacred writings." Instead, they came together and agreed that the stamp of God's hand was obvious on certain books.

It did take more time for a few New Testament books to be agreed upon than others. Serious debate took place on only five of the twenty-seven New Testament books that we now have in our Bible. In the end, the Church agreed that those five books were also divinely inspired.

I hope this appendix has helped you understand why the books in the Bible today are the ones God intended us to have. You can be certain that what you are reading is, in fact, the inspired Word of God. It was tested by the early Church and found true. The writings of the Old and New Testament are what God intended the church to have.

[1] I am grateful for the work of Gordon Fee and Douglas Stuart in their book, *How to Read the Bible for All It's Worth,* for some of the information on classifying different Psalms contained in this section.

[2] Nashville: Thomas Nelson Publishers, 1995, p. 1033.

[3] Compiled from Ladd's *New Testament Theology*, Gundry's *Survey of the New Testament, New Testament Survey* by Tenney, *Dictionary of Jesus and the Gospels* by IVP, *NICNT commentary on Mark, Matthew Henry's Commentary on Mark, The Hermeneutical Spiral* by Osborne, *How to Read the Bible for All It's Worth* by Stuart and Fee, *The New Illustrated Bible Dictionary, The New Testament World* by Malinga, and my own thoughts.

[4] Quote taken from the *NIV Application Commentary. The Book of Acts*, by Ajith Fernando. 1998, p. 25.

[5] Quoted in *The Book of Jesus*. Ed. By Calvin Miller (Nashville: Broadman & Holman), 1996.